the moment

*A Practical Guide
to Creating a Mindful Life
in a Distracted World*

Achim Nowak

Foreword by Faisal Hoque

New Page Books
A division of The Career Press, Inc.
Pompton Plains, N.J.

THE MOMENT
EDITED BY LAUREN MANOY
TYPESET BY KARA KUMPEL
Cover design by Amy Rose Grigoriou
Printed in the U.S.A.

To order this title, please call toll-free 1-800-CAREER-1 (NJ and Canada: 201-848-0310) to order using VISA or MasterCard, or for further information on books from Career Press.

The Career Press, Inc.
12 Parish Drive
Wayne, NJ 07470
www.careerpress.com
www.newpagebooks.com

Library of Congress Cataloging-in-Publication Data

CIP Data Available Upon Request.

acknowledgments

I am deeply grateful for the selfless guidance and support of so many cherished colleagues and friends during the writing of this book.

Dana Newman—for believing in this material and so expediently finding a home for it.

Faisal Hoque—for sending me to Dana in the first place, and for your magnanimous support every step of the way.

Adam Schwartz, Kirsten Dalley, and the entire team at New Page Books—for your faith in this manuscript, and for treating it with such care.

Donna Ratajczak—for once again elevating my work with your impeccable editorial wisdom.

Irene Borger—for the wonderful conversations I get to have with you. They were the springboard for this book.

Sally Fisher—for teaching me how to do the transformative work.

Leandra Campbell and Kathy Heffner—for being my backbone at INFLUENS. Without your diligent research and fearless behind-the-scenes work, this book never would have been written.

Rob Doucet, Allison Dykstra, Blair Glaser, Meredith Porte, Robyn Stratton-Berkessel, Frederick Tan, and Stefanie von Fallois—for so generously sharing your stories with me.

Suzanne Daigle, Sue Elliott, Jameson "Flash" Maroncelli, Robyn Stratton-Berkessel, Liz Reynolds, and Jo-Aynne von Bourne—for reading various iterations of this manuscript and challenging me to get clearer and clearer.

Richard Sankar and Suzanne Daigle—for opening your beautiful homes to me. Your spirit lives in the pages of this book.

My devoted Energy Boost readers—your responses to my Boosts stimulate me in more ways than you can possibly know.

Mother Meera, Gurumayi, and Eric Butterworth, for opening the doors to my heart.

And my mom, for loving me as I am.

contents

foreword

Most of us are taught from a very young age onward to desire success. Success—the quest for it and the act of chasing our goals and dreams—can be a potent personal animator. We exert effort. We work hard. We hustle, hustle, and hustle some more. And if we are fortunate, we're rewarded with the tangible gifts of our efforts.

And yet, even during those times when the ride feels exactly like the exhilarating thrill we thought it would be, we have the occasional moment when we realize that all we're really doing is working hard. We're not so sure we are actually enjoying the pace of the ride. We're not even sure we got on the right ride, in the first place. Moment by rushed moment, we have this eerie sense that life is slipping away from us.

Our eye is intently focused on the finish line, while life is happening now. This "now" is flying by at lightning speed.

Living in the moment doesn't mean we don't care about the future. It means that when we make the choice to do something, we focus solely on the act of doing it, rather than letting our mind wander into the future or the past.

In college, at my janitorial graveyard shift, I had a supervisor who used to remind me every night to "be kind to the floor, buff her carefully—and then see how well she shines." At those particular moments, nothing else mattered—only the shine on the buffed floor. It taught me to lose myself completely in an utterly mundane task. Being in the moment allows us to escape from adversity and conserve our inner energy.

For a fast-paced entrepreneur like me, perhaps the most paradoxical lesson has been around the need to slow down to move forward. Slowing down is a deliberate choice that can lead to greater appreciation for life and a greater level of happiness, which yields better results in one's endeavors.

In the context of mindful living, slowing down does not imply taking a vacation every other month. It is what we must practice every day. It means taking the time to do whatever we're doing. It means single-tasking rather than switching between a multitude of tasks and focusing on none of them.

Several decades ago, the term "mindfulness" used to imply Eastern mysticism related to the spiritual journey of a person who follows the teachings of Gautama Buddha. Buddhists believe that being "well, happy, and peaceful" comes from practicing mindful living. Today, from self-help gurus to business leaders, from scientists to politicians, many talk about mindfulness. And the scientific community now believes that by practicing daily mindfulness, we can take advantage of the neuroplasticity of our brains and thereby improve the state of our lives. William James was one of the first psychologists to address the notion of neuroplasticity, back in his groundbreaking 1890 text *The Principles of Psychology*. The central idea behind neuroplasticity is that our brain can restructure itself based on our perception and experience.

the moment

In my book *Everything Connects: How to Transform and Lead in the Age of Creativity, Innovation, and Sustainability* (McGraw Hill, 2014), my coauthor and I wrote:

> Bishop, the Canadian psychologist, supplies us a useful two-component definition of mindfulness: regulating our attention to maintain a focus on our immediate experience, and approaching the phenomena of our experiences with curiosity, openness, and acceptance regardless of how desirable we find those phenomena to be.
>
> Mindfulness allows us to have a more nuanced, articulate understanding not only of the events happening outside of our bodies but of those happening within them.

When we are mindful, we begin to be a more objective witness of our own experiences: When placed into a situation where we would normally become aggravated, we can observe our aggravation as it arises. As a meditation teacher once told me, without mindfulness we are reaction machines. But with mindfulness, we give ourselves some room to move. Instead of acting out of our long-held tendencies, biases, and patterns, we can act in a way that serves the situation and serves the people involved.

These personal outcomes have major conse-
quences for organizations, as well. If innovation and
growth is something that arises from being able to
see the same set of data in a new way, practices that
allow us to approach new situations with a fresh, un-
biased, and slightly less conditioned state of mind
are an asset. If we rely on our colleagues to share
the things that cure our blind spots, practices that
deepen our relationships are an asset. If we need to
translate long-term goals into daily actions, practices
that allow us to introspect with more accuracy are an
asset. If we simply need to better navigate the stress-
ful stimuli of our days, we need all the tools we can
get.

This is where the practice of daily mindfulness
enters the picture. It shows us how to begin to stay
more conscious in the present moment. It teaches
us to do so in the midst of a rapid pace that may, at
times, be beyond our control. It also helps us to discover ways of slowing down so we may better savor
life while it unfolds, moment by moment.

It's been said that the only two jobs of a Zen
monk are sitting *zazen* (meditation) and sweeping.
Cleaning is one of the daily rituals of a Zen monk,
one of their most important daily practices. They
sweep or rake, and they try to do nothing else in that
moment. The next time you're doing housework, try
concentrating on the housework—on the dust, on

the motion, on the sensation. Cooking and cleaning are often seen as boring chores, but actually they are both great ways to practice mindfulness—something I ritualistically try to do at least once or twice a week. Sounds simple, but it's actually pretty hard. Go ahead and try it.

I believe mindful living can be practiced in many forms.

When I look at the literature we have available to us on how to best live a mindful life, it seems to fit into two distinct buckets. On one hand, there are wonderful books that focus on one particular mindfulness practice—meditation. They offer instruction on how to start a meditation routine, and they plumb the infinite richness of what is revealed during the act of meditation. Many of these books are steeped in a particular spiritual or religious practice.

On the other hand, we have books that urge us to seek enlightenment and abandon the shackles of an ego-driven life. Meditation figures into the mix, but it is merely a small part of a much bigger story. The quest-for-enlightenment books remind us that our ego enslaves us to a life of illusion. True inner peace will only manifest once we fully rid ourselves of our attachment to the false life we lead.

The Moment walks a refreshing middle path between these two seemingly opposing takes on the mindful life. Achim Nowak draws on the wisdom he has gained in more than 20 years of practicing Hinduism, with a steady commitment to meditation and the gifts of chanting. But he also incorporates what he knows from years of training actors at top US acting schools, and what he has learned during a decade of leading personal transformation events in HIV/AIDS communities. He also references his exceptional expertise in helping senior business leaders from around the world to be more fully present. *The Moment* is blessed by a multidisciplinary voice. It takes us on a robust, highly practical, and nonmystical journey into the mindful life. That is one of its many shining assets.

The book's subtitle leaves no doubt about what we're in for. This is not a tale of mindfulness as a private activity. This is a book that squarely places you and me, the readers, into the world—our encounters with people, places, and things. Many of us yearn to live more fully in the moment. We don't always know exactly what that means or what it may look like.

Achim offers us four keys to more fully experience any moment. I am struck by how simple but profound these keys are. This is in many ways a back-to-basics book. It reassures us that we're already whole and don't need to work harder. Instead of learning new techniques that require constant practice, we rediscover what we instinctively knew as children. We explore the pleasures of "unworking" and allowing ourselves to return to a state of childlike delight.

Faisal Hoque

Faisal is the founder of Shadoka and author of *Survive to Thrive, Everything Connects,* and several other books.
Follow him @faisal_hoque or visit FaisalHoque.com.

the
moment
begins

the moment begins

Helen at the Airport

I walked into the Hudson News Booksellers at LAX's Terminal 3 and picked up a New York Times. *As I stood in front of the cashier and poked through my wallet to pull out some dollar bills, I sensed a man standing next to me. I looked up. There he was. I felt a jolt in my chest as I looked at him. The man gulped and held my gaze. I saw a tenderness in his eyes. There was a simmering silence between us.*

As I handed the dollar bills to the cashier, the man asked me: "Would you like to grab a cup of coffee?" I felt another jolt. And just then a voice on the loudspeaker announced that my flight was boarding. I grabbed my change and looked at him and said: "That's my flight." His face seemed to suddenly fall. I saw a flash of sadness in his eyes.

I shoved the wallet into my purse and hurried down the hall to my gate. When the airline attendant took my ticket I looked at her and blurted out: "I was in the bookstore just now and I met the most wonderful man." "Well, you have to go back and find him!" she said. She was firm in her command.

So I ran back to the bookstore.

The man was gone.

This is my friend Helen Miller's story. Helen relays it to me as we sit around her cozy Santa Monica kitchen table, nibbling on feta-stuffed olives and crackers and heaps of hummus.

Helen had a moment at LAX.

It had a clear beginning, middle, and end.

It stood out from the moments before. It would inform the moments that were about to come.

I hear the wistfulness in Helen's voice as she speaks. Yes, Helen had a moment. It was a moment that slipped away.

What if it had not?

What about all of the other moments in our lives that simply get away because we are distracted, because life is moving too fast? What if there were a way of knowing a moment more fully, more deeply, more quickly as it unfolds? How might this alter the experience of our lives?

Augenblick

Every second of every day, moments are waiting to be born.

We either notice or we don't.

Consider the German term *ein Augenblick*. It is a well-known expression with multiple meanings. The literal one goes something like this: *within the blink of an eye*. And there is the colloquial meaning, used on a near daily basis by most Germans: *Wait a moment, I'll be right there*.

The German language also has a more literal match for the English word "moment," *ein Moment*. But the allusions of *ein Augenblick* are the ones that cut to the core.

Within the blink of an eye a moment can happen.

Within the blink of an eye we may notice.

Within the blink of an eye the world can change.

Within the blink of an eye it can all slip away.

Helen knows. You and I know. That is the beauty and the terror of a moment.

We might as well belong to the tribe that yearns to catch the blink, don't you think?

The Offering

"Just live in the moment."

We have all thought the thought. Most of us have uttered the words. It's a wonderfully appealing notion, isn't it? As enticing as it sounds in theory, the idea of living in the moment is also fast becoming the ultimate mindfulness cliché.

What the heck does it actually mean?

What happens in a moment? How do we experience a moment? What is it that we notice when we notice? These are some of the questions we will have a little bit of fun with in this book.

This is not a book about simply being more spontaneous or "going with the flow."

It is more.

It is not about learning how to better meditate.

It is more.

It is not about the Buddhist notion of having a beginner's mind.

It is more.

The Moment is fueled by a few simple beliefs: As we more richly know our moments, we invoke a more richly lived life. A richly lived life is a more momentous life. And a more momentous life is an inherently good and desirable thing.

the moment

In the pages that follow, we will go for a walk on the wild side with our conjoined twins, memory and meaning. The more keenly *we remember* and the more courageously *we make meaning*, the more memorable our life becomes. "The least of things with a meaning," Carl Jung asserts, "is worth more in life than the greatest of things without it."[1] And memory, like it or not, is always in the mix. There is no new moment without the echo of other moments. There is no blank slate. Neutral doesn't exist.

Four keys will open the doors to our momentous life. These keys are simple. That is their beauty. They are common sense. They're also great fun.

As we explore the four keys together, let go of any notion that this is hard work. While you flip through the pages of this book, do not think of it as learning something new. No, you are remembering something that you have known all along. *The Moment* is a return to a state of childlike delight, when all of our moments were brazenly lived.

It is that simple. It is that rich.

Gurdjieff Made Me Do It

When I was 25, I was determined to fully live every single moment. I had discovered the writings of George Gurdjieff, and I was instantly smitten. Gurdjieff is an early 20th-century mystic from the Caucasus who sought to understand the nature of reality and the hidden meaning of life. He believed that most of us spend our life in a state of hypnotic "waking sleep." Gurdjieff also suggested that through a series of rigorous exercises, we could reach a higher state of consciousness.[2]

I surely did not wish to be a sleepwalker. I wanted higher consciousness. So I created my own little Gurdjieff experiment.

I lived in a studio apartment at 1512 Corcoran Street, in the Dupont Circle area of Washington DC. It was a fourth-floor walk-up that required me to navigate several flights of elaborate stairs. This was my daily Gurdjieff assignment: Instead of hustling up the stairs to my apartment as efficiently as possible, I decided to slow down and fully experience the mundane.

I was going to explore the reality of walking up to my apartment.

I took each step of the stairs with great deliberation, one at a time. Tentatively. Slowly.

the moment

I saw the silver metal strips that capped the edges of each step.

I surveyed the ziggy-zaggy cracks and the small and not-so-small crevices in the dark plastered wall that lined one side of the stairs.

I gazed at every rod in the black metal railing that flanked the other side, paint bruised and chipped.

I noticed the dust that had coalesced into tiny mounds of dirt at the far edges of each step.

I traced the murky light of the fluorescent overheads as they threw shadows on the walls.

It took me up to 45 minutes to reach my apartment. I did this for 10 days.

It was a very slow climb.

I saw the details. I noticed. I noticed some more.

And it signified nothing.

The climb up the stairs was just the climb up the stairs.

It did not lead me to a higher state of consciousness. The ascent had no desire to be memorable. Stair-climbing at 1512 Corcoran Street simply was not a momentous act. I gave stair-climbing the royal treatment, and I discovered, floor by floor, that not every moment wants to be a royal moment. Whew. What a relief!

This was my first Gurdjieff experiment. And my last.

Marge in Havana

It is 6:40 a.m. in Havana, and I slide into a rickety rusty-white chair next to my friend Marge Schiller.

Marge is gazing at the sea. Behind us, the lawns of the Hotel Nacional are lulled into a deep morning slumber. From the terrace at the base of the slope, we survey the curve of the Malecon promenade and the El Morro fortress in the distance. The Gulf of Mexico glitters with a steely grey sheen.

"I'm into the experience of experiencing," Marge declares, a satisfied grin on her face. "Listen to the symphony of sounds." Marge cocks her head heavenward as she speaks. Her silvery white 76-year-old pixie hair thrusts away from her head, as if it were listening too.

"Seven different kinds of birds," Marge recounts. "There is the sound of a car driving by. Then silence. Music blasting from another car. A flag flapping in the wind."

She pauses. Another silence, and I slink into the seductions of this morning. A whiff of mariposa jasmine ascends my nostrils. I sense the outline of Marge's body next to mine, pressing into the back of her chair, sitting still. I have walked into her moment. It is ours now.

Marge is a renowned thinker in the world of "appreciative inquiry," a conversational framework that organizations use to create better futures.[3] A key tenet of appreciative inquiry is that as we look at any situation, we might as well begin by appreciating that which is strong, that which is good, that which already works. Notice that which we may have taken for granted. Notice what has always been there, right in front of our eyes.

"When I am fully present," Marge explains, "I absorb experience with every sense. That is the only way I can truly understand the world."

Yes, with absolutely every sense. That's where the appreciation of a moment begins, doesn't it? I had called on my senses during the Gurdjieff experiment of my youth. It didn't seem to matter. This morning, in a special place, with a cherished friend, it does.

Havana at 6:40 a.m. It starts in a moment such as this.

There Is No First Time

Do you have places you return to again and again? The sort of places that fill your heart with anticipatory joy, even before you are there? Because you know you'll get to canoe across the cool waters of Blue Mountain Lake again. Get to sneak a bite of your favorite fried green tomatoes at Sally Jean's Cafe, get to screech with silly abandon on the Astro Orbiter, watch the sun set over Shelter Island with a melon mojito in hand.

These are the places where we go to re-create moments.

Chances are, the very first time you set foot in one of your places, you may have had an inkling, a feeling that you have been here before.

Here is a place of mine. It is just before 7:00 a.m. I slip out of my orange MINI Cooper convertible at the Greene Street parking lot in Hollywood Beach, Florida. Saunter up a narrow wooden walkway that cuts through a mangrove thicket. The mangrove trees rise high alongside the planks and then loop in tightly wrung spirals above the path. They create the illusion of a shaded tunnel.

As I walk into this tunnel, I feel like I am entering a magic passageway. It leads me to a secret world. Just where the planks reach a plateau and the path flattens, the secret world reveals itself. A set of handrailed stairs descends to a deserted beach. Royal palms rise majestically on either side. And in front of me a view of the Atlantic bursts open wide, as if I could see to the ends of the world.

The first time I amble up the wood planks to Greene Street Beach, I am instantly transported. These planks are the very same planks I walked in my summers on Fire Island, a few hours outside of Manhattan. The weather-beaten wood. The rusted nails that no longer pin anything down. The bounce in the planks as my flip-flops press in. The light that pulls me to the ocean. The skip in my heart as I anticipate the sea.

These are my memory triggers. My joy magnifiers. My sensory umbilical cord to the magical summers of my Fire Island past.

"Experiences are encoded by brain networks whose connections have already been shaped by previous encounters with the world," Harvard psychologist Daniel Schacter writes in *Searching for Memory*. "This preexisting knowledge powerfully influences how we encode and store new memories."[4]

The first time I swing into Independence Drive in Provo, on the Turks and Caicos Islands, I notice the low stone walls that line this road.

"It reminds me of Mallorca," I say to my friend Richard Sankar, who is driving us.

That afternoon, Richard and I stroll past the same stone wall and hang a left at the sign for property BE3. A pebbled path cuts through a thicket of brush toward the beach.

There are no wooden planks here, no fancy railings, no royal palms. But I turn to Richard and say: "It reminds me of Greene Street Beach."

It is my first time in Turks and Caicos.

There is no first time in Turks and Caicos. There is no first time on Greene Street Beach.

There never is.

The shaded tunnel, the magic passageway, the opening to a secret world: That is the little story I tell myself as I saunter up the Greene Street planks. Or to be precise, it is the story that presents itself to me. It supercharges my experience of the experience. It is my very own Greene Street Beach myth.

After all, it's just a walk up a set of wooden planks.

There is never just a walk up a set of planks.

And there is no first time. There never is.

The Thrill of Slipping through the Gate

Form is no different from emptiness.

Emptiness is no different from form.

Form is precisely emptiness.

Emptiness is precisely form.[5]

These words are found in the beginning of the Heart Sutra, one of the best-known Buddhist scriptures of all times.

In Sanskrit, the Heart Sutra is called the *Prajna paramota sutra*. *Prajna* means "real wisdom." *Pra* means "before or prior to" in Sanskrit, and *jna* means "knowledge or knowing." So *prajna* describes an intuitive way of knowing. A wisdom that has nothing to do with intellectual knowledge.

Cognitive psychologists explain how we make meaning by rigorously examining any new experience. We compare the new experience to our current world view, assimilate the experience if it fits, and consider a different perspective if it doesn't. Meaning making is viewed as a deliberate cognitive process.

And it always happens after the fact.

Prajna wisdom, however, reveals itself as a moment unfolds. It is instant, and it just as instantly illumines our experience of a moment.

Helen's encounter at LAX, a moment graced with prajna.

When I think of my earliest memories of prajna, I flash back to a moment from my childhood. It stands out because it is laced with the joys of instant wisdom. It is connected to an impossibly beautiful place in Turkey: Tarabya.

And because it is a memory from a long time ago, this thought also crosses my mind:

I could be making this all up. It could be that it never happened this way at all. It could be that it's simply a beautiful story.

It could be. But I don't think so.

Between the ages of 10 and 14, I lived in Ankara where my dad was assigned to the German embassy. In summer, folks from the embassy migrated to an old Victorian estate in a village right on the Bosporus strait, halfway between Istanbul and the Black Sea.

Tarabya.

The estate, 15 acres deep, sprawled into a U-shaped mountain ledge that wrapped itself around a level plain. It housed a smattering of gilded white mansions and featured a central promenade lined with tennis courts and fountains and a faded swimming pool. Walking paths threaded into the mountain and offered ravishing vistas of the Bosporus and

Asia beyond. Everything in this estate spoke of a grandeur that was no more, white paint peeling on doors and verandas, weeds that had cracked the clay tennis courts. The front of the property lined a narrow winding road that ran alongside the Bosporus. A gargantuan black wrought-iron fence shielded the estate from this road and the world.

Ten years after my last visit to Tarabya, I saw a movie by the great Italian film director Vittorio de Sica, *The Garden of the Finzi-Continis*.[6] It told the story of a wealthy Jewish Italian family who lived in an opulent villa, circa late 1930s, shielded from the rest of the world by a magnificent walled-in garden. I watched it spellbound by flashes of memory, thinking of Tarabya. And so the memory loops go.

Tarabya was my garden.

To enter the estate from the street I would slip through a crack in the iron gate. When a car pulled up, the attendant would swing open both wings of the gate. The remainder of the time, he just opened a little crack. Outside of the fence, a steady stream of cars cruised down the Bosporus road. Fishermen sat for hours on a mini pier. Families lounged on beach chairs and listened to transistor radios. Vendors with carts sold melons and chips and cola. It bustled.

My slip through the crack took mere seconds. It filled with me with an extravagant joy every time. It was my slip from a public world into a private one. From the anyone-can-travel-here road into a privileged realm. From a wide-open space into a sheltered one. From a loud world into silence.

Just some of the levels of meaning in that little slip. I might not have named them quite that way when I was 11 and 12. But it was oh, so clear to me I wasn't merely going from one location to another. I knew.

The thrill of the moment transcended the performance of the act.

Life connoisseurs cultivate the art of such rapid meaning making. They crave their moments of instant wisdom. The quick illumination, the unexpected aha. The thrill of knowing. The slip through the gates of meaning.

Let us be life connoisseurs, shall we!

The Empty Space

A few decades ago, when I did nothing but direct theater plays, Peter Brook was my hero of heroes. I no longer direct. He still is my hero—Peter Brook, one of the great visionary theater directors of the 20th century. In 1985 I attended an all-night performance of Brook's legendary staging of the Mahabharata at the Brooklyn Academy of Music. It was 9 hours long. A troupe of actors from every part of the world, together on a crumbling old stage. A timeless epic tale, a performance reimagined, brimming with life.

To create great theater, Brook said in his book *The Empty Space*, we do not need marvelous sets or stunning costumes or brilliant lighting. Those are the artifacts of "dead theater."[7] No, to create great theater, all we need is actors and an empty space.

In the performance of our everyday lives, you and I are the actors. Every moment is the empty space.

Nothing happens in this space. Everything does. It is that simple.

We decide.

Marina Abramović is arguably the most influential performance artist in the world today. Fans like Lady Gaga prance nude through the woods in a promotional video for Abramović's future institute in upstate New York. Jay Z's music video *Picasso Baby: A Performance Art Film* was inspired by his encounter with Abramović during her 2010 retrospective at the Museum of Modern Art.

Detractors have called her a fame whore. Love her or hate her, fame has come to Ms. Abramović for a reason. She is ferociously reimagining what happens in the empty space.

Abramović's performance at the Museum of Modern Art was named *The Artist Is Present*.[8] During the 10-week run of the show, Abramović sat motionless in a chair, 6 days a week, 7 hours a day, looking straight at whoever sat opposite her, waiting for moments to happen.

As I jot down these words, her new show *512 Hours* just opened at the Serpentine Gallery in London.[9] The chair, Ms. Abramović has since decided, is too much of an artifact. The gallery is entirely empty but for a row of lockers where visitors can deposit their bags and electronic gadgets. Several museum guards are present, and Ms. Abramović.

Empty. And no one knows what will happen in the space.

"That is the point," Ms. Abramović tells the *New York Times*. "The idea is that the public are my material, and I am theirs. I will open the gallery myself in the morning and close it at 6 p.m. with my key. I want to understand how I can be in the present moment, be with the public."[10]

What an exquisite reminder. The space is always empty. Every moment is always waiting to be born.

Here is where you and I enter the frame. Yes, in the performance of our everyday lives, you and I are the actors. Let us reimagine how we consciously and boldly inhabit our empty space. Every day, moment by moment. The Buddhist might say, be still; surrender to stillness; hear the wisdom within. The artist might say, go and create in the empty space; it is your canvas of possibility. I suggest we do both.

The pages that follow introduce us to four keys. These keys will be our guide. They are disarmingly simple. They are entirely common sense. And in the spirit of Peter Brook and Marina Abramović, they are also wickedly playful. That is their beauty.

Key #1: Awaken the Senses

As we more keenly know all of the senses, we uncover a more sumptuous experience of the world. We look at how actors train to be more sensually attuned. We investigate the connection between the senses and emotion. And we celebrate the moments that brim with layers of sense memory.

Key #2: Crave Meaning

As we activate our ability to instantly know meaning, we discover a deeper appreciation for moments as they unfold. We become mindful of how *prajna* talks to us. We notice how meaning shows up within the mini beats of our days. And we clearly see how the stories we tell ourselves inform the meaning we find.

Key #3: Wave-Ride Energy

"Wave riders" are folks who sense the energy of a moment and choose to ride the wave. As we seize the energy of a moment, we experience the thrill of momentum in our lives. We discover how moments of discomfort propel us into life-changing "aha" moments. And we appreciate the power of extreme events, when circumstances unfold so rapidly that we have no choice but to ride the wave.

Key #4: Make Time Stand Still

Two fundamental choices make time stand still: We slow down, and we fully surrender to present activity. We observe how practices like meditation and the chi disciplines facilitate a slowdown. We find a new appreciation for the ordinary and the mundane. And we see how the moment we fully immerse ourselves in any activity, we are rewarded with the experience of flow.

The beauty of deploying the four keys? The notion of time suddenly no longer matters.

We are more fully in the here and now.

That is the ultimate beauty of a momentous life.

key
number
one

key #1:
awaken the senses

What Is There All the Time

If you've never done it, try it. It doesn't matter where you do it. It will work anywhere.

Lie down on the floor and close your eyes for 5 minutes. Not to meditate. No, lie down and listen to the sounds you hear. If you are concerned about knowing when 5 minutes have passed, set an alarm.

Take a breath. Listen.

Voices of people—distant, faint, close by. Voices in your head, perhaps. The trilling of birds. The growls of other creatures. This is what you're likely to hear. The din and roar of cars. A child screeching in the distance. Pipes rustling. Technology clicking and clacking. The whistling of a breeze. The rustling of a leaf.

There may be a hum in the air, the kind of low hum that makes you think, what the heck is this? And even as you ask the question, you know you will not get the answer.

It matters not. Consider it the big mysterious hum of life.

Oh yes, and you may hear your heart beat. Your mind may wonder, am I feeling it or am I hearing it beat?

Again, it matters not. You sense it. You feel it. You hear it. You notice.

Most of the time, we have the illusion of being in the moment. We're not in the moment. We're on a heavily filtered mind-trip. The trip takes place in a high-security cabin in the frontal lobes of our brain—our thought bunker, a place that happily ignores much of what is actually happening in the moment.

There is nothing inherently wrong with the mind. At its best, our mind is a springboard for brilliant creative thought.

Just 5 minutes, however, will pull us out of our minds, remind us of all that we miss, all the time, when we're convinced that we are in the moment. And all we did was listen. Imagine the other sensory markers we never notice as we revel in our impoverished moments.

Does it matter that we hear the bird sing? The voices in the distance? Does it matter that we sometimes miss them?

That's for us to discover.

Being out of our minds is a darn good place to begin.

What Actors Know

I admire great actors. Meryl Streep, Dustin Hoffman, Morgan Freeman, Edward Norton, and Vanessa Redgrave are a few of my favorites.

They seem vibrantly alive. Kinetically charged. Über-human.

Actors inhabit a condensed hyperreality in which lives are parceled into 30- or 60-minute television chunks, 120-minute movie journeys, 180-minute theater extravaganzas. In actor reality, each moment matters. And I'm not talking about the moments of high drama, the fits of laughter, the welling-up-with-tears moments.

No. Especially in a moment of stillness, a moment of seeming insignificance, a great actor seems in tune with absolutely everything—his limbs, his thoughts, his sensations, and everything that is happening around him.

A special few have an innate ability to be fully alive at the drop of a dime.

Everyone else goes to acting school. That includes Meryl Streep, Dustin Hoffman, Morgan Freeman. Yes, my entire gang of favorites; they all studied acting. And the first thing they did in acting class? They sharpened their five senses.

Think of our eyes-closed-lie-on-the-floor activity. Now think of months and months of doing such exercises, for every one of your senses. Eating an apple that isn't actually there, recalling the tart taste of this apple, bite by bite, in your mouth. Handling an object, eyes closed. Sensing each nook and cranny on the surface of this object. Sensing texture, sensing weight. Facing away from the door as your teacher brings in plates of food, each food item with a distinct aroma. Without turning around, you smell the foods that are paraded past your back.

These are sensory isolations. They focus on one sense at a time. The moment we add another human being into the frame, the information input gets a heck of a lot more complicated. Allison Dykstra, TV producer for hit sitcoms on Comedy Central and HBO, describes an exercise from her first year of studying acting in the Sanford Meisner Program at the Elizabeth Mestnik Acting Studios in Los Angeles.

"I am facing a partner," Dykstra explains, "and we both have our eyes closed. When we open our eyes we say the first thing that comes to mind. We keep looking at our partner, and we keep repeating that first phrase."

Sounds simple, doesn't it? Well, in this "simple" exercise, both individuals are responding to multiple sensory stimuli. Seeing. Hearing. And the impulse that comes from within.

Why the repetition, you ask?

"My acting partner said to me, 'You have beautiful eyes,'" Dykstra explains. "Simple, right? It took me until the 15th time before I actually got what he was saying. *Oh yes, I have beautiful eyes.* That's when I finally had an internal reaction to the words."

It was a moment from the moment it began. It was a richer moment when the words actually landed.

This, of course, is laboratory life. In real life, we rarely make it to round 15. We simply don't notice what is coming our way, what our reaction is. We stumble from one non-moment to the next.

This is why actors train the senses—to get it right away, every time. To get it deeply. You and I are the actors in our own lives. Each moment we experience happens on our very own movie set. In a world that increasingly inundates us with too much sensory information, it's tempting to simply shut down. Wouldn't it be nice if you and I could get it in the first round as well?

We can.

Actor training is life training. And it is fun to boot. Some actors choose acting to chase fame and fortune. But most actors get hooked on acting way before fame and fortune ever come their way. They get seduced by these early explorations.

Hooked because they discover life.

How Sense Memory Works

Outspoken, fierce, indefatigable: Meet Sally Fisher, one of the early AIDS evangelists in the United States. Sally fought for dignity and quality of life for folks with HIV/AIDS back in the late 1980s, when the cause wasn't fashionable, the outlook bleak.

Sally developed a program called the AIDS Mastery. Over the course of a weekend, participants went on a personal journey to discover ways of living an impassioned life in the face of changing life circumstances.

Powerful stuff. I became one of Sally's Mastery facilitators.

Here's a chat we had at the start of every program. I call it the chair chat. If you have ever attended a personal-growth program, you likely had your own version of the chair chat.

This is the easy part of the chat: I pull up a chair, any chair, in front of the group. We describe what we see. The shape of the chair. Curved legs, straight legs. Arm rest or perhaps not. The material the chair is made of—wood, lucite, chrome. The color. The sheen. Any other particular markers. A piece of lint on the chair. A special stitch. A knob.

That is the chair. Anything else about the chair—it's a pretty chair, it's an ugly chair, it's a clunky chair, it's an elegant chair, I like this chair, I can't stand this chair, I would never buy this chair—is mind chatter. It is arbitrary and has nothing to do with the chair. The chair is just the chair.

Simple, right?

Most of our life moments are not concerned with the chair. We think we have a moment with the chair. We are full-throttle engaged in our chatter about the chair.

Now here's where our chair chat may get surprising.

You look at this chair. You see just the chair. No mind chatter going on. Yet suddenly, you feel a wave of emotion sweep through you. A wisp of sadness, perhaps. A ripple of joy.

Where the heck did that come from? you wonder. The chair is still just the chair, right?

Welcome to sense memory. It is one of the reasons why actors so rigorously train their sensory capacity. You have just experienced the connection between a sensory cue and emotion.

Here's how sense memory works: Let's say you remember a beautiful moment in your life. The moment you married your spouse, perhaps. The moment was supremely vivid for you while it unfolded, and at the same time a blur because your heart was awash with emotion. As you think back on this moment, you find yourself zeroing in on a few little things. The smile on your spouse's face. The glow of love in his eyes. The sound of the harpist as she finishes the final chord of "Amazing Grace." The late afternoon light as it flitters across the lake.

And the red kerchief. It juts out of your spouse's lapel, perfectly folded, tipping to the sky. You see the kerchief, vermillion red, and you feel yourself well up with emotion again. The very same emotion you felt during the ceremony. Extravagant, overflowing.

The kerchief is the cue that pulls the emotional trigger.

A small sensory cue, a seemingly insignificant detail, is the link to a vast experience.

Why do you feel the wave of emotion as you look at the chair which is just a chair?

It could be the curve in the front legs of the chair, the cobalt-blue velvet of the cushion, the piece of rust on the metal frame. They could be the sensory link to other moments, other chairs—the invisible thread that invokes the emotion and connects you to the richness of your life.

Yes, a kerchief is rarely just a kerchief. A chair is rarely just a chair.

The Layers of a Moment

There are moments, and there are moments on steroids. Consider the senses your steroids—but healthy, legal, good for you.

A March morning. I pull out of Bahia Honda State Park in the Florida Keys and head north across the Seven Mile Bridge. The top on my new turquoise MINI roadster is down. Balmy gusts of wind whip through the car. The sky is an iridescent pale blue, the late-morning sun is caressing my neck. Hozier is singing "Take me to Church" on the Marathon radio station.

It happens in a quick second. I feel my heart burst open wide. It bursts because of the blue that is everywhere, the ocean, the wind. I flash back to a moment of driving across this bridge with my mom, in my old orange MINI, top down, Mom's hair flapping in the breeze. I flash back to driving across the bridge with my friend Jameson Maroncelli, just after leaving a languid morning at Bahia Honda. I flash back to sitting in a darkened movie theater in Bonn, Germany, with Mom and Dad, watching *True Lies*.[1] Relishing the movie's big chase scene in which Arnold Schwarzenegger and Jamie Lee Curtis race toward a cliffhanger on the Seven Mile Bridge. Mom leaning in to me and whispering "We've been there." I hadn't been there yet.

Such are the layers. My March morning ride across the bridge would have been a glorious moment without the layers. It is more sublime because of them.

Do not confuse a memory flash with living in the past. Norma Desmond in the movie *Sunset Boulevard* lives in the past, in her glory days, in all that is no more.[2] In Norma's case, not a good thing. Living in a present that is illumined by its threads to the past is an entirely different matter. My ride across the Seven Mile Bridge transcends the pleasures of the immediate moment. It celebrates the continuity of my life. Integrates it.

It's whole.

The sensory cues all around me invoke this wholeness.

Not every moment needs to be a moment on steroids. Sometimes I look at a chair and all I see is a chair. But how sweet it is when the layers reveal themselves.

Here's a little sushi analogy. Indulge me, please.

I love sushi. I have eaten sushi all over the world. Some of it sublime, much of it not. Bad sushi tastes like a one-flavor facsimile of fish. What's on my plate looks like a rainbow roll. I see the slices of tuna and salmon and yellowtail and bits of shrimp wrapped around a funnel of seaweed and rice. I remember what I should be tasting, but all I actually taste is one big blob of nothingness.

the moment

Now here's a taste of a great rainbow roll. With each bite a new sensation springs to the fore. The warm texture of loosely bonded rice. The firm prickle of the nori sheet. The finely shredded crab inside the rice, wet with a wisp of spicy mayonnaise. The creamy, buttery glide of yellow tail across my tongue. The dense chewy bite of the tuna. The sea smell of the shrimp. The slippery gleam of the salmon.

Each bite yields a delicious surprise. And another. And one more.

That is the gift of sensory layers.

A great moment is like savoring a sublime rainbow roll. I have accepted that I'm not going to have scrumptious sushi all the time. But when I do, it just tastes so good.

I like the layers.

In my sushi. In my moments.

The Prerequisite

Think of sensory awakening as the graduate school of life.

Everyone is admitted. Admission is free. There are no tests, no exams, no interviews. But to thrive in grad school, there's a prerequisite.

Dr. Barbara Brennan is one of the world's leading authorities on energy healing. In her now classic bestseller *Hands of Light*, Brennan delineates the many ways in which we block energy.[3] Think of energy as life that longs to come to us. Because we have been wounded in the past, we prevent this energy from getting in.

We keep life at bay. We block it.

Brennan describes 6 different types of bodily energy blocks and 20 different types of energetic defense systems. Energy wants to move through us, in and out. When we have been hurt at a certain stage in our lives and have not had a chance to express this hurt, we start to hoard emotional pain. This pain morphs into body armor that we wear every day. It festers in our groin, our abdomen, shoulders, elbows. Energy no longer moves. In addition, we resort to energetic defense systems when we don't feel safe in our environment. We withdraw. We throw verbal arrows. We become hysterical. We suddenly feel "beside ourselves."

the moment

"My acting teacher took one look at me," Allison Dykstra explains with a chuckle as she describes her very first Sanford Meisner class, "and said 'You'll need to get rid of your Superwoman shield.'"

Because most of us habitually block, we each wear our own version of the Superman or Superwoman shield. And because that is what we know, the person we are with this shield feels like who we are.

The price we pay? In the spirit of self-protection, we don't see the glint of the sun. We don't notice the stranger's smile. We don't spot the butterfly that dances across the meadow. We don't hear the hum of life.

We repel moment after moment. We live a shadow life.

So here's the prerequisite: Go on an archaeological dig. Remove the blocks. Release your accumulated hurts. To make room for a more richly lived life, you gotta tear down a wall or two. The most effective digging is done with the help of a seasoned archaeologist—a therapist or energy healer who has been trained to find the specific location of your body wounds and is able to help you extract the pain.

Evict the debris of the past. Get it out.

Archaeological Digs

I had my first excavation when I was 22. I was a dubious cynic. It felt like voodoo to me. I didn't quite understand how it worked. Still don't fully understand. But I know it works.

Joy McLean Bosfield was my voice teacher. She received her students in a slender row house on Upper 16th Street, just north of Malcom X Park in Washington DC. The lessons took place in a tiny room at the top of the stairs, Joy always standing behind the piano, the student across from her, doing vocal scales. Joy hailed from the original cast of *Porgy and Bess*. By the time I found my way to Joy, she was well into her seventies, a regal apparition with an impossibly erect posture, her upper body sheathed in the blue angora turtlenecks she so loved, adorned by a thick white pearl necklace, hair pulled into a tight chignon.

"Breathe from your penis," Joy would say to me every week as I was attempting my scales.

I became a highly competent penis breather. My singing, however, remained atrocious. A year later, Joy threw in the towel.

"Your jaws are too tight," she announced with a defeated look on her face. "It's your German upbringing. There's nothing else I can do for you. I am sending you to Dr. Richardson."

My German jaws, my body armor: They prevented me from properly breathing. More significantly, they kept me from fully experiencing my life.

Dr. Richardson was a hypnotherapist with a small office in the far northeast corner of Washington DC, a part of town that white boys in the 1970s never got to visit. He became my first block remover. During my six sessions with Dr. Richardson, I lay on a massage table in his backroom. Light filtered in only through half-drawn shades. The remainder of the room was unlit, as if I were a character in a scene from a sinister film noir. My eyes remained half open. Dr. Richardson sat behind me. I sensed him but I didn't see him; I just listened to his deep sonorous voice as he taught me how to talk to my jaws. Talk them into relaxation. Deep relaxation. Relaxation beyond my conscious mind control. Each session was a further lesson in learning how to hypnotize myself.

I knew it had worked when, 9 months after my final hypnosis session, I was in a gymnasium with a group of fellow actors on a Tuesday night, rehearsing for a production of *A Midsummer Night's Dream*. We were sprawled on the gymnasium floor, doing our vocal warm-ups, when I suddenly heard the sound of my voice as I was vocalizing. The sound startled me. I felt like I was hearing myself for the first time. My voice had a rich, guttural sound, a raspy resonance it had never had before. It came from way down deep.

It buzzed and vibrated in my forehead, well past my jaws.

Block removed.

There are many roads to removal. Hypnosis is a relatively gentle path. My visits to Dr. Richardson were not my only excavation. Primal screams, pounding pillows, core energetics, rebirthing: These are more active, less benign approaches to excavating old pain. Go and find the approach that makes the most sense to you. And remember, the best archaeologists will offer you more than the occasional cognitive insight or a place where you can have a good cry. They dive deep down into the body wounds with you.

You may think to yourself, gosh, this sounds so thoroughly unpleasant. Why the heck would I want to go on a dig?

Digging is your investment. Here's what you get in return. Do you run or swim or do yoga? If you do, think of the moment right after you stop the activity. You are breathing fully, deeply. Your body is richly oxygenated. Adrenaline is pulsing through your veins. Corny as it sounds, your entire body feels alive.

As you look up you see the familiar outlines of your exercise room. The blinds that shield the interior from the sun. The rack with the free-weights. The treadmill. Everything looks just as it did when you entered the space. Yet it all seems to flicker with a brighter light.

Sharper. Bolder. Richer. Luminous.

Like a lucid dream.

It is what happens when we temporarily bypass the blocks.

Now imagine that you have engaged in a little bit of digging. Torn down a ruin or two. Did some permanent removal. Here's your return.

Brighter. Sharper. Bolder. Richer. Luminous. All the time.

Funny thing is, the world was luminous all along.

Dolphin Tales

"Did you hear the tray that just dropped?" Stefanie von Fallois asks me. "The laughter of the people at the table behind us? The child who's squealing in the pool?"

Stefanie and I are sitting poolside at the swank Biltmore Hotel in the Coral Gables suburb of Miami. Stefanie, a psychologist, talks about sensory filtering.

"You and I hear these sounds as background noise, and we are able to focus on the conversation we're having. People with severe trauma have their filtering mechanisms broken down. They hear everything, see everything, sense everything. They become totally overwhelmed."

Stefanie knows. She helps patients for whom the senses have become too much to bear. Soldiers who have returned from war with severe psychological trauma, women who are victims of sexual abuse. Patients diagnosed with PTSD, with dissociative personality disorder.

Stefanie is a therapist who works with dolphins. Her clients travel to Curacao in the Caribbean for 10 sessions of therapeutic dolphin interaction. They ride dolphins, dive with dolphins, connect with the dolphin spirit.

the moment

"How does this work?" I ask Stefanie. I have accompanied Stefanie for a day of dolphin work, observed her as she is immersed in water, guiding her clients to interact with a dolphin. But I long to better understand what actually transpires in the moment when a dolphin and a human meet.

"There have been numerous studies," Stefanie says with a shrug. "Nobody has been able to fully pinpoint what happens in this encounter. We just see a clear shift in a client's behavior."

This is the hypothesis: Think of the dolphin as a perfect embodiment of female and male energy. A smooth, soft surface coupled with supreme physical strength. A playful spirit. A protector. The dolphin approaches every person without fear. You can hold on to a dolphin and he will take you on a journey. You will experience motion in water. You will experience the safe surrender to another force, another form. You will sense the energy of this powerful mammal.

All of this happens in water. A highly sensual place. Our original state.

The touch of the dolphin, literally and symbolically, extracts our pain. Releases it into the ocean. The dolphin becomes the conduit to our original way of being.

This is not a cognitive experience. It's a supremely sensual one.

With Stefanie's clients, the senses are the problem. The senses are also the answer.

"Smell is the oldest of the senses," Stefanie tells me. "We work with smell a lot."

Before a soldier is sent into water to play with a dolphin, he is asked to briefly smell something that is pleasurable for him. Suntan lotion, perhaps. Cologne. A cigar. A sea shell. He decides.

When this soldier leaves Curacao after his 10 dolphin sessions, he leaves with a survival kit, an actual satchel that he will now carry with him at all times. The satchel is full of his survival items—the things he smelled before he played with a dolphin. For a soldier who is partial to auditory stimulation, this may also include a tape with sounds of a dolphin splashing in the water.

This kit is used in a disarmingly simple way. When a solider feels a wave of flashbacks coming on, he reaches into the kit and takes a whiff of one of his pleasant-smelling items.

He returns to his dolphin state.

Stefanie explains, "I had a female client, Elizabeth. As a young woman, Elizabeth had been systematically raped over a period of years. When I say years, I mean hundreds of times. By family members. Absolutely brutal. Elizabeth's trauma was so severe that she could not crawl into bed at night. She would lie on the floor of her room and curl up. We gave her a T-shirt with a picture of her dolphin printed on the front. Wearing this T-shirt, Elizabeth was able to sleep in her bed again."

At bedtime, Elizabeth returns to her dolphin state.

That is the power and the essence of the dolphin moment. The encounter with the dolphin reminds us of who we really are, deep down, before life became unbearable.

It is our return to a sensual world.

When the senses have become the problem, the senses are also the answer.

They are our way home.

Sensory Tripping

It is 3:00 in the morning. The avenues are empty.

I speed from the far reaches of northeastern Washington DC toward Georgetown and Key Bridge in my mom's well-worn beetle. I am 21 years old.

There is no traffic, but the world outside my car is teeming with life. The oak trees that line the avenues gyrate as if they have a beating heart. The pavement pulses and contracts while my car seems to fly across it. The night sky roils, and I feel like I'm watching a fast-forwarding loop of the sky. My heart is pulsing as vehemently as the road.

Motion, everywhere. My car is in motion. My insides speed like my car. The world around me is in a dual-state of hypermotion and slow motion, all at once.

I have just spent 4 hours in the ballroom of a private mansion, standing on a balcony overlooking a dance floor, sipping acid-laced lemonade that dripped from a fountain.

As I crawl into my bed in Arlington Towers early that morning, I glance at my bedroom ceiling and continue to see the roiling sky. Clouds swirl and recede. Light bursts across a rain-drenched field, deep saturated greens, golden honey shafts of light. An army of desert dunes reaches to infinity, shifting, undulating. Vistas. More. Endless.

If you have tasted hallucinogens, you have your own version of this story. For quite a few folks, a moment on steroids equals a moment with a stimulant. A trip into a hypersensory wonderland in which time no longer matters and a mind-expanding version of reality reveals itself.

Most Native American cultures use mescaline or a variant as part of their sacred rituals. Aldous Huxley famously wrote about his experiments with mescaline in his 1954 book *The Doors of Perception*. Our normal doors of perception, Huxley asserts, are sheltered by our beliefs about what is real and the limited language we use to describe this reality. Our filters. These filters limit what we are able to observe. Hallucinogens are a quick bypass to such filters. They temporarily open the doors to offer us a glimpse of what Huxley encapsulates in the phrase "the vast cosmic mind-at-large."[4]

In the 1960s, the joke goes, folks took LSD to make the world look weird. Now we take Prozac to make the world look normal.

Easy joke, I know. The yearning for the hallucinogenic is the yearning for a more fully sensed life.

The hope that beyond the pitter-patter of our daily doings, there is more. The fervent desire to know transcendence.

It is a sacred yearning.

I know that this yearning can be quelled, day in and day out, without the use of a stimulant. This book explores some concrete ways in which you and I may open our doors of perception. Meditation, yoga, and conscious breathing are just a few of the physical practices that expand our experience of the world daily, habitually. Not merely in the special moment where we take a vacation from everyday life. No, all the time, with no temporary bypass.

Howard is a fellow who belongs to the I-will-take-nothing-at-all tribe of earthlings. A boisterous, big-hearted man, Howard spent a good chunk of his early adult life indulging in the modern-day street variants of a stimulant—meth, Ecstasy. Until they brought him to his knees.

"It is such a joy for me when I wake up in the morning," a now sober Howard explains, "and I am fully here. There is no buzz in my head. No extra pulsing in my veins. No quick rush of any kind. I just have this sense of stillness as I look out of my bedroom window in the morning and take it all in. The smell of the wet grass. The balmy breeze that swoops up from the canal. The sound of the clock ticking next to my bathroom door. The photo of my favorite mandala on the nightstand beside my bed. That is all the connection to the divine I need."

I smile as Howard speaks. *He gets it*, I think to myself. After all the hustle-bustle and all of the distractions, we rediscover our simple delight in what is there, in front of us, right here, right now. It is a child-like delight. Sweet. Unfettered. It is how we first knew the world, many moons ago, before we grew up and life became complicated.

This simple appreciation is the heart and soul of living in the moment.

And it starts with the senses. Always. Their beauty. Their simplicity. The infinite ways in which we know them.

Alive.

Explorations for Key #1: Awaken the Senses

A vibrant way of being in the moment begins with a more robust experience of the five senses. I trust it is evident by now that learning to fully savor our senses can be a truly delicious experiment. Here are some ways in which to explore.

Take an Acting Class

If the notion of taking an acting class appeals to you—and heck, even if it intimidates you a bit—run out and find a class. In any major urban center you likely have a reputable theater company or acting studio just around the corner that offers theater training.

There is absolutely no wrong class that you can choose. Actor training is life training. For the purposes of our explorations in Key #1, any class with a special focus on improvisation or theater games will be especially beneficial.

Regardless of the class you pick, you will discover ways of more fully "tuning in" to any moment. You will more richly appreciate the surroundings you're in. You will more acutely connect with another person. And most important perhaps, you will become more intimate with yourself.

I mentioned that it will be fun, right?

Conduct Sensory Exercises

Go and create your own sense isolation exercises. Just like the first exercise at the start of this chapter, keep your exercises short and sweet. 5 minutes, no longer.

To sharpen your listening, create opportunities to keep your eyes closed. Sit on your balcony. In a city park. At the beach. If you don't trust yourself to keep your eyes closed, use a blindfold. Just listen.

To sharpen your sight, focus on one object and only one object for a while. Your desk. The trunk of a tree. A car. A moving cloud. Your eyes will be tempted to flitter about. Resist. Focus on color, on shape, texture, movement. Observe the infinite visual richness of just one object.

To sharpen your touch, select a few objects that have distinct surfaces and textures. A rubber glove. A hammer. A sponge. A scrubber. A metal pan. Lay them out on a table. Normally, we handle these objects in fleeting seconds. Time yourself. Handle each object for a minute. Delight in the very different ways in which your hands experience each item.

To experiment with smell, go to an ethnic neighborhood in your city. Little Italy. Little India. Chinatown. Stand outside of a restaurant kitchen and simply inhale the smells. Or conduct your own dolphin experiment, no dolphin required. Identify four or five smells that you really like. Get the items with those smells. Take a few minutes and saturate yourself in their smells, item by item.

To experiment with taste—yes, go and eat some food! But eat it without the usual distractions. No texting, no watching the news. Be brave and eat a meal on your own, without talking to another person. Eat it slowly, and give your undivided attention to the experience of chewing, sensing, tasting your meal.

Do a Little Digging

Do certain parts of your body habitually feel tight? Do stress and tension quickly grab a hold of you? Do you have a sense that you may be holding on to lots of accumulated pain from your past?

If you answer yes to any of these questions, there's a good chance that you are moving through life with some body armor. This body armor inhibits your experience of the world.

Be bold and release the blocks. Do this with the help of a professional you trust. A hypnotherapist. An energy healer. A rebirthing practitioner. A Rubenfeld synergist. There are many ways of going on a dig, but the most liberating work happens in and through body excavations.

the moment

Think of it this way: short-term investment, long-term gain. A deeper and more delicious appreciation of all the senses will be your reward.

key
number
two

key #2:
crave meaning

When a Moment Screams Meaning

Jordan Spieth leads from the start.

He never stops leading, never lets any other golfer get closer to him than three after his first round. Squarely ahead of the pack. And the pack at the 2015 Augusta National includes Phil Mickelson,

Rory McIlroy, Justin Rose, Tiger Woods. Exceptional company.

Spieth breaks record after record at this tournament: the youngest player to lead after the opening round; the most birdies for the tournament at 28; the 36-hole record at 14-under 130; the 54-hole record at 16-under 200. And on Sunday, April 12, after having shot a record-tying 270 (18), Jordan Spieth becomes the 2015 Masters Champion at age 21.

In a postvictory press conference, Spieth says: "This is arguably the greatest day of my life. And to join the club that is the green jackets and to join Masters history and put my name on that trophy and to have this jacket forever is something I cannot fathom right now."[1]

Jordan Spieth is having a milestone moment.

It screams meaning.

Meaning amplifies our experience of a moment. It places it squarely into the larger story of our life, even if much of that life is yet to unfold. We may not know how the story will be written, but we have a keen sense that this moment, the milestone moment, will alter the script. Yes, a milestone wears its meaning on its sleeve—or in this case, its green jacket.

It's an easy moment, in a way. The meaning of a 2015 Augusta National win is blazingly clear. The Masters is not just another golf tournament. This is not just another win. Every participant in the 2015 Augusta National trains rigorously to compete at this level. Intense preparation and fierce anticipation amplify the meaning of a Masters win. Most professional golfers never get to don the green jacket, never hold a Masters trophy. Spieth's comments reflect his keen awareness of the historic dimension of the day.

Meaning gets more complicated when we don't get the prize. It's less obvious for Tiger Woods, who was the Jordan Spieth of a decade ago. Tiger is not even close to a win in 2015. It's less obvious for veteran Phil Mickelson who comes in second to upstart Spieth, Mickelson's 12th second-place finish at the Masters. Is second place a loss or an outstanding ride at the Masters? Are 12 second-place finishes a losing streak or a sign of consistently exceptional performance?

"There is only the meaning we each give to our life," Anaïs Nin writes in her celebrated diaries. "An individual meaning, an individual plot, like an individual novel, a book for each person."[2]

A trophy is just a trophy, right? After all, who decided that winning at the Augusta National is all that important anyway? Well, the moment we choose to play the competitive-athletics game, a victory has meaning. When we decide to play the I-want-to-get-married game, the moment your spouse slips the ring on your finger has soul-tingling impact. When we play the I-want-to-get-a-great-education game, the moment we march in our graduation ceremony has life-altering significance.

Instant milestone meaning.

Clear meaning, however, does not always equal clear emotion.

Consider Bruce Jenner's moment of triumph at the 1976 Olympics, winning the Gold Medal in the decathlon. In Jenner's gender-transition interview with Diane Sawyer—Jenner's final interview as Bruce—Sawyer takes out an iPad. Together they look at a quick montage of Jenner in competition, culminating with a clip of him standing on the podium, holding his trophy up high. Sawyer asks Jenner to describe what he sees.

> Jenner: "I'm a confused person at that time. Running away from my life. Running away from who I was."
>
> Sawyer: "With fear?"
>
> Jenner: "Big-time fear. Yeah. Yeah. Uhhm, scared to death. Didn't know what my future held at the time."[3]

Did Jenner actually feel this fear during his moment of triumph? Standing on the podium, hoisting his trophy for the cameras? Or is his statement to Diane Sawyer a convenient trick of memory as he recomposes the story of his life? I surmise the latter is true. We'll never know.

There is the meaning that we intuit as a moment unfolds. There is the meaning we discover with the passing of time. As you and I look at how we may more fully experience our moments, we focus squarely on the insight that reveals itself in the here and now.

Yes, prajna wisdom. The beauty of instant knowing.

It shouts in a milestone event. It whispers the rest of the time.

How We Know

July 1992. I have just returned to Manhattan after a year of living on the remote island of Tobago. In Tobago I did nothing but windsurf and read every post–World War II British novel I could find in the island's only public library. I became an impassioned windsurfer, but after a year of living on a tiny island, I missed New York City. Terribly. I missed the honking of taxis. I missed the summertime stench of trash emanating from the garbage bins. I missed the smell of exotic foods wafting out of kitchens as I walked down the street.

I also return to Manhattan totally broke. I had been a successful theater director and acting coach in this city, but that life had proved too workaholic for me. I need a job. A different job. At once.

One morning, I find myself sitting on the #5 train, heading from the East Village to downtown Brooklyn for a job interview. And I think to myself, your life is really going down the toilet when you're reverse-commuting to Brooklyn to get a job. This is the pre-hipster-glorified Brooklyn of the 1990s. I walk into 50 Court Street for my appointment. When I get off the elevator on the fourth-floor offices of the Victim Services Agency, my heart further sinks. The walls of this office are painted a drab and dreary beige. The chairs in the waiting area are wobbly and frayed at the edges. Everything looks shabby and rundown and in dire need of repair.

I want to run out of there immediately.

When it is time for my interview, I am guided to a little room at the end of an even drearier hallway. This room has no windows, no decorations, just two chairs and an empty desk. A woman rises from one of the chairs and shakes my hand. Lynne Hurdle-Price. Her grip is firm. Her smile radiant. Her dreads seem to bounce with a giggle as she speaks. Lynne's energy fills the entire room.

Within seconds I know: Crystal clear. No doubt. I want to work for this woman. I have just found my new boss.

A moment of prajna.

This is how prajna talks.

A voice. A whisper. A sudden sense of calm. A neon sign blinking at us. An unexpected mental connection between disparate thoughts. *Oh, it all makes sense now.* A stellar inkling that this moment, this situation, this social constellation is right. That it is wrong. An undeniable visceral sensation. A sudden lifting of a mental cloud.

A clear knowing. A feeling of peace.

It is easy to trivialize the prajna moment by calling it a hunch. A whim. I like indulging my whims.

the moment

I like a sense of whimsy. I enjoy whimsical things. Prajna is none of this. It is not a temporary flight of fancy. Prajna settles on us like a blanket of certainty. It comforts. Under its cover we take a long inner exhale. *Oh yeah, got it.*

And it requires no mental effort. There is nothing to analyze, nothing to figure out.

We don't work for prajna. Prajna comes to us.

When wisdom is sweet, it tends to add a sense of quiet rapture to the experience of a moment like a nice sip of cognac—a warm glow in the chest, a sweet settling. When wisdom is bitter, it has the power to change every second that follows. Do you remember a moment when you knew that you were with the wrong person? When he finally said the wrong thing once too often? No one will ever talk to me that way again, the inner voice in your head screamed. I simply can't listen to this crap anymore. This is the last time. I got it. No more. This is it.

Prajna.

A sudden drop into wisdom. Sometimes the drop lasts a mere second or two. Sometimes its impact is felt forever.

Shocking how often we ignore it, isn't it?

The Stories We Tell Ourselves

Beware of the stories you tell yourself. They are the meaning you will find.

Our beliefs are embedded in our stories about the world: The essence of all human life is love. The world is an evil place. The ego is the source of all human struggle. The true purpose in life is to be of service to others. Liberation from suffering leads to enlightenment. The happiest people are those who don't take life too seriously and know how to have fun. Our true calling in life is to better know the divine.

Each story informs the prajna that shows up for us. And each story, in one fell swoop, tempts us to ignore the evidence that doesn't fit.

Religion offers a narrative about creation, purpose, and the rituals that create a connection with the God-force. If you're an atheist, your antireligion narrative is your story. If you're an enlightenment seeker who believes that all stories about the meaning of life are an ego delusion, that's your story.

You have a story.

In the United States, we like our stories sunny side up. The You-Can-Be-Anything-You-Want-To-Be story. The Life-Is-An-Abundant-Universe story. The We-Are-All-Equal story. The Things-Will-Work-Out-In-The-End story.

I, too, like my sunny stories. They beat the alternative. But what sort of prajna shows up when we are surrounded by unfathomable evil?

"If there is meaning at all," Viktor E. Frankl wrote, "there must be meaning in suffering."[4]

In 1942, Frankl, a prominent Jewish psychiatrist from Vienna, was arrested by the Nazis, transported to the Theresienstadt ghetto and subsequently taken to the Auschwitz and Dachau concentration camps. Frankl's pregnant wife and his parents didn't make it out of the camps alive. Frankl did. In his bestselling book *Man's Search for Meaning*, published in 1946, Frankl doggedly pursued this question: How do we find meaning in the face of such vile behavior against humanity?

Frankl's answer is resolute. The prisoner who finds sustenance in the simple everyday moment, the small act of kindness, the prisoner who maintains faith in the possibility of a future beyond the current circumstances, is far more resilient than the one who despairs.

Frankl tells of an insight he has during a particularly harrowing night, as he and a group of fellow prisoners are herded by Nazi guards across rough mountain terrain:

A thought transfixed me: for the first time in my life I saw the truth as it is set into song by so many poets, proclaimed as the final wisdom by so many thinkers. The truth—that love is the ultimate and the highest goal to which Man can aspire. Then I grasped the meaning of the greatest secret that human poetry and human thought and belief have to impart: *The salvation of Man is through love and in love.* I understood how a man who has nothing left in this world still may know bliss, be it only for a brief moment, in the contemplation of his beloved.

A moment of prajna under duress. I am moved by the depth of Frankl's insight. In a setting so void of kindness and compassion, during a very dark night of the soul, Frankl hears the voice of love.

A drop into universal meaning.

Who Says Father Knows Best?

When I think of Frankl, I think of the great myths that exist in cultures all over the world. Myths are our hyperstories, if you will—classic, archetypal, larger than life. They ascribe meaning to the rites of passage we encounter from the moment we arrive on this planet. Mythologist Joseph Campbell's research convincingly shows how similar the myths from cultures around the world truly are. His famous telling of the hero's journey captures some of the classic stages found in many myths: The hero hears a call to adventure, meets with a mentor, finds allies, faces challenges, resists temptation, endures a dark night of the soul, is resurrected, becomes a servant to others.[5]

If this sounds a little Hollywood to you—well, it is. Hollywood has famously co-opted these mythic storylines and turned them into dashing adventure movies. *Star Wars*, anyone?

Why is a myth helpful in the act of meaning making? A mythic view of the world offers prajna during a time of distress. *Aha. Got it. Not just another bad day. No, it's a rite of passage to the next phase of my life.* A myth also instills in us a sense of awe about the world. We appreciate that not everything is what it seems to be. We understand that there are larger hidden forces that animate the universe.

Wonderful. And a myth is still just a story. Beware of the stories you tell yourself. They define the meaning you will find.

Consider this ancient Indian fable.

One day, the father of a very wealthy family took his son on a trip to the country with the express purpose of showing him how poor people live. They spent a couple of days and nights on the farm of what would be considered a very poor family.

On their return, the father asked his son, "How was the trip?"

"It was great, Dad."

"Did you see how poor people live?" the father asked.

"Oh yeah," said the son.

"So, tell me, what did you learn from this trip?" asked the father.

"I saw that we have one dog and they had four," the son answered. "We have a pool that reaches to the middle of our garden and they have a creek that has no end. We have imported lanterns in our garden and they have the stars at night. Our patio reaches to the front yard and they have the whole horizon.

"We have a small piece of land to live on and they have fields that go beyond our sight. We have servants who serve us, but they serve others. We

buy our food, but they grow theirs. We have walls around our property to protect us, and they have friends to protect them."

The boy's father was speechless.

Then his son added, "Thanks, Dad, for showing me how poor we are."[6]

Be a Beatnik

That moment was one big blur.

This whole day felt like one big blur.

The entire 1990s are one big blur to me.

Time parameters vary, but at one point or other many of us have uttered a statement such as these.

In a blur, nothing stands out. Life runs on and moments run together. One moment folds into the next. The architecture of our lives disappears. Catching prajna in a blur is like trying to catch a ray of sunshine in a monsoon.

I am an architect's son, and architecture matters a great deal to me. I grew up studying the blueprints of the buildings my dad was building. I would sprawl on my bedroom floor for hours at a time and scour every detail of a blueprint—the width of the walls, the swing of the windows, the placement of the electrical sockets, the flow from one space to the next. I consider a blueprint the secret language of a house. It determines how a house rises, how it functions, how it will feel to be inside that house.

Just as a blueprint is the secret language of a house, beats are the secret language of our lives. They are the architecture that contains our moments.

the moment

A beat, first and foremost, marks the passing of time. Our heart gives the original beat. *Kathump.* Again. Again and again. And again. In music, a beat connotes a clear underlying pulse or rhythm. This pulse tends to change over time. Sometimes it does so spontaneously, as in jazz; or in the case of an orchestral performance, the rhythm changes according to a meticulous plan.

When you recall a specific day, portions of that day may feel a little frenetic. Others may seem to lumber. Yet others seem to positively crawl. These are the rhythmic shifts within a day. Its distinct passages. Your beats.

Most of us organize our days via a calendar or date book. They list the obvious beats. Meeting with Joe for an hour. Beat. Lunch with Adriana. Beat. At the gym for 45 minutes. Beat. These are the formal beats of a day, readily observed, easily marked.

Why do beats matter? Wisdom doesn't reveal itself in a blur. The only meaning of life in a blur is that life is a blur. Wisdom shows up in the beats.

If you want meaning, you gotta notice the beats.

There are beats within a beat. While I grab lunch with my friend Adriana at the deli down the street,

I stumble into a series of mini beats. Adriana and I have known each other for more than 15 years. We have lots of history, lots of ups and downs between us. Sometimes I enjoy Adriana's company, sometimes I get exasperated by her need to talk incessantly. As we munch on our turkey and swiss cheese sandwiches, no mayo, sweet peppers, extra pickles, we reminisce about a road trip we took to Las Vegas a few years back. Adriana and I didn't get a lot of sleep on that trip. We partied. Hard. A little too hard. We laugh uproariously as we recall one of our more wicked transgressions. Beat. Adriana and I groan as we discuss the staff meeting we just left, in which our vice president of sales gave the same tedious pep talk he gave a week ago. Beat. We both choke up as we contemplate the fate of our much-loved colleague Burt who was laid off, just this morning, out of the blue. Beat.

In a movie, every scene is a beat. Every scene has meaning. That's why the scene is included in the movie in the first place. In our daily life scenes follow scenes, just as they do in a film. But many of our scenes seem to have no apparent significance at all. We are simply busy doing what we are doing that day, engaged in what this day has put before us.

Just fine. And then, once in a while, a scene jumps out.

While I lunch with Adriana, as we're in the midst of recalling an especially salacious detail of our transgressive night, it suddenly hits me: I have a bunch of great friends. I often have terrific times with those friends. But as much as Adriana can sometimes annoy the heck out of me, I don't think I have this much fun with anyone else. Ever. How brilliant!

It is just lunch with Adriana. And it is blessed by this exquisite insight.

The beauty of my Adriana-lunch-meaning? I don't have to stop and reflect in the middle of our lunch. *Hey Adriana, let me pause for a moment and figure out the meaning of this lunch; I'll get right back to you.* No, it just presents itself.

You desire meaning? Become a beatnik. Notice the beats. Notice the change from one beat to the next. Notice the beats within the beats.

Wisdom will come.

Double-Track Your Moments

Imagine, for a moment, that you are on a dance floor. The DJ is spinning your favorite beat. Lights swirl in an even flicker across the crowd. The sound is bold, insistent, yearning. One by one, bodies around you submit to the pulse of the song. They swivel. They swoon. Arms weave the air. Hands pull torsos closer. You too feel your limbs begin to shake. Like every bone in your body is beaming a giant grin.

You're having fun. And then, for a moment, your brain kicks in and says, *Wow, I'm having fun!*

That's double-tracking. You're having an experience, and you are conscious of having the experience. When our brain says to us, "Wow, I'm having fun," it does not yank us out of the experience our body is having. On the contrary, the observation helps us to savor the moment. It fuels further fun.

Meaning can be as simple as "I'm having fun." It can also be more trenchant.

Our ability to double-track is especially helpful in a moment of stress and anxiety. You sit in a planning meeting to help refine your firm's next strategic plan. Everyone present was told to come to this meeting prepared, to review the current plan and bring ideas that will focus next year's plan. The moment you hunker down in the conference room, sip your latte, and begin to cut and paste out of the existing document, listen to the tweaks proposed by your colleagues, the inevitable tweaks that have been regurgitated at every executive meeting all year; as you fail to hear a single new idea that will inject vitality into this plan, and a palpable lack of enthusiasm fills the room, a little voice in your head pipes in, loud and clear: *This is a tired strategic plan that will never work.*

Double-tracked.

The moment in which you hear the voice in your head becomes its own mini beat. *This is a tired strategic plan.* A double-tracked moment as a meeting drones on.

The beauty of this beat? Because of your insight, you now have a choice. You can accept the dynamics of this strategy-review gathering and the likelihood of a not very compelling outcome. Or you may speak up to alter the course of the meeting.

We don't get the gift of choice without staying conscious.

There is a fine line between double-tracking and mind chatter. A double-tracked moment is graced by keen insight into the experience we're having. This insight is quick and clear. It offers an instant understanding of the deeper dynamic of the moment. *These people never have any new ideas* is mindchatter. *I hated last year's planning meeting, and this one is just as bad. I don't know why for a second I thought this would be a livelier meeting. We're incapable of having productive planning meetings.* Mind chatter. With lots and lots of stories behind it.

Chatter is just chatter. It isn't prajna. Beware of your stories. They get you into trouble, most of the time. When you choose them well, they steer you into moments of sheer delight.

Micro-Moments of Love

On a cloud-soaked September afternoon, I pull up to a toll booth on Interstate 95, just outside of Naples, Florida. "Hold on a minute," I say to my friend Sandy Lawson whom I am chatting with on the phone. I roll down my car window and hand my $3.00 to the clerk in the booth. She is a woman of a certain age, wearing a pair of oversized sunglasses, radiating good cheer.

Me: "You look like an Italian movie star!"

Clerk: "Don't I wish." She giggles as she stretches my crinkled dollar bills into submission.

Me: "Maybe you are. Maybe you're here, doing research for your next great movie role."

My toll booth friend laughs out loud with unabashed delight. I beam with pleasure at her joy.

"Boy," Sandy says to me on the other end as I pull away from the booth. "You just made her day!"

A moment. Beginning, middle, end. Fleeting. Fun.

Yes, it is all that, but to me it is more. I think of my toll booth exchange as a micro-moment of love. That is my secret meaning. And my stranger with the big bold shades and I have created this micro-moment together.

I like the notion of a micro-moment of love. If I'm going to tell myself a story, this is the sort of story I like.

Barbara Fredrickson, PhD, coins the phrase "micro-moment of love" in her compulsively readable book *Love 2.0*. Frederickson is the director of the Positive Emotions and Psychophysiology Laboratory at the University of North Carolina in Chapel Hill. In *Love 2.0*, Fredrickson steers our understanding of love from its big romantic connotations toward a deeper appreciation of the simple, everyday moment. The moment that radiates shameless positivity. Because that's what a micro-moment of love does.

"Within micro-moments of love," Fredrickson suggests, "your own positivity, your own warmth and openness, evoke—and is simultaneously evoked by—the warmth and openness emanating from the other person." [7]

Here's how a neuroscientist explains it. Uri Hasson at Princeton University conducts speaker-listener research about how two brains get into sync. He calls this process "neural coupling." This coupling is the means by which two people understand each other. In his findings, the key area of the brain that shows coupling is the insula, an area linked with conscious feeling states. In other words, neural coupling is much more likely to occur when you and I feel a shared emotion. When my joy meets your joy, joy magnifies. When my playfulness meets your playfulness, more play erupts. When my love of others meets your love of others, a micro-moment is born. And you and I feel, even if just for a fleeting moment, deeply connected.

My stranger at the toll booth—playful neural coupling. And the best part of this encounter? I know it is a micro-moment of love as it unfolds because that is the experience I am intentionally creating. Yes. Instant meaning, cocreated with a stranger whom I will never see again.

As my colleague Robyn Stratton-Berkessel and I chat about micro-moments of love, I appreciate how fully Robyn embodies positivity and a deep desire for connection, the very qualities that Barbara Fredrickson champions in her book. Robyn, keenly curious and full of quizzical insight, is a positivity strategist whose mission in life is to instigate positive organizational change.[8] She tells me of an incident in a supermarket. This incident, ironically, took place on Valentine's Day.

"I was standing in the checkout line at the supermarket," Robyn explains, "and the fellow just ahead of me was short 58 cents when it was his time to pay. Well, I dug into my purse, pulled out some change, and passed it on to him. He thanked me profusely, and off he went. Just after I had stowed my purchases in the trunk of my car and climbed into the front seat, a man ran toward the car and started to bang on the window. It was him. When I rolled down the window he handed me a bouquet of tulips. He was a florist, it turns out, and the trunk of his van was filled with flowers he was delivering." And with a huge and wistful sigh, Robyn adds, "I was so touched by that. It meant so much to me that it was meaningful to him."

An unexpected act of kindness in the supermarket line inspires another unexpected act of kindness. Of course Robyn was touched. That tends to happen in a micro-moment of love. What makes this exchange a micro-moment of love? You get to decide. I get to decide. The florist gets to decide. Robyn gets to decide.

And the gift of the flowers? How lovely that on Valentine's Day, they were given not to celebrate a romantic union, but a simple ordinary act of love. Sweet.

"A micro-moment of love literally changes your mind," Fredrickson explains. "It expands your awareness of your surroundings, even yourself."[9]

Micro love is fleeting. But within the moment, biochemical changes occur inside of our brains. The impact of these changes transcends the brevity of the moment. Their ripples are felt way past the moment at the toll booth, in the supermarket. Anywhere.

Meaning is the caviar of life. Sometimes it discovers us. Sometimes we run for it, arms open wide.

Cultivate a meticulous meaning mindset. Learn your own secret prajna language. Learn it well. That is how meaning finds you.

And if you believe in the story of micro-moments of love, then by all means, run for such moments. Run for them, arms open wide. Create them. Micro love will suddenly be all around.

Prajna moments are quick. Micro love is ephemeral. But oh, how such moments enrich the experience of our life.

Who says love is complicated?

Explorations for Key #2: Crave Meaning

We have been conditioned to make sense of our lives by taking a pause, reflecting on an event that occurred, figuring out how it relates to our story about the world. If the occurrence fits, we tend to have a sense of relief. If it doesn't, we are challenged to view it as an exception or possibly adapt our world view.

There is great value in making meaning after the fact. Life connoisseurs, however, are masters of sensing and knowing meaning as a moment unfolds. Prajna. It doesn't show up all the time, but when it does, watch out. Prajna powerfully fuels our appreciation of any moment we're in.

Here are some ways in which you may wish to explore your experience of prajna:

Hear Prajna Talk

Because prajna is the wisdom that comes to us from our unconscious minds, start to observe how your unconscious communicates with you.

Does it talk to you via an inner voice that whispers? Does it talk to you by showing you a clear picture or image, like the answer to a secret question? Does it steer you toward a place, an event, a person where something happens that illuminates an inner question you have? Does it show up via a strong sudden emotion that washes over you as if out of nowhere? Or does certainty take hold of you with an instant sense of calm?

Pay attention to the unspoken signals you receive, at all times. Have fun discovering this secret inner language of yours. Because not all signals may be significant, you get to decide which ones "make sense" and "feel right," and which ones may be a mere passing whim.

Remember that constant mind chatter is NOT prajna. True wisdom, regardless of the form in which it presents itself, shows up as a clean, distinct signal, separate from what precedes it and from what is about to follow. That's why we notice. It's a concise communication. Mind chatter is constant noise.

Become a Beatnik

The main beats of our lives are neatly laid out in our daily, weekly, monthly calendars. Meaning tends to reveal itself in mini beats within these larger beats.

We are more likely to receive insight by choosing to double-track our moments. Have an experience and stay conscious of the experience. Fully engage in your activity and observe it at the same time. Prajna is more likely to reveal itself.

When you are in the middle of a beat, stay mindful of the underlying musical language. Your beat may shift into different moods. Different speeds. Different emotional colors. Notice the shifts. And know that during the shifts, prajna is more likely to reveal itself.

Prajna is not a given, it's a gift. But as you begin to practice the art of double-tracking and observing the shifts from one mini beat to the next, the gifts will be given.

Five Stories I Tell Myself

It is impossible to have stories about the world. Some of our stories are based on what Mom or Dad told us, what our teachers have instilled in us, what our minister at church reinforces every week. Some of our stories may hail from a specific spiritual practice we have chosen for ourselves as adults. Others may be the result of simply living life—the successes, the loves, the hurts, the losses, and the meaning we have derived from it all.

Some of these stories will be crystal clear to you. Others may be floating around in your subconscious mind.

Because the stories we tell ourselves define the meaning we find, take a moment to jot down the five stories that are most compelling for you. Jot them down quickly, without overthinking the exercise. Distill each story into a sentence. This distilled sentence describes a belief you have about the world. *We live in an abundant universe. We live in a dog-eat-dog world.*

Be honest with yourself. Write down the stories that you truly believe deep down, not the ones that you would like to believe but are actually a little cynical about.

As you look at your list, ask yourself the following question:

Is this the meaning I wish to find?

And consider these two questions in follow-up:

If I could remove a story or two from my storybook, what would they be?

If I could add a story or two, what would those be?

The moment we become conscious of our stories, we become conscious of the meaning we find. And meaning is the caviar of life.

key
number
three

key #3:
wave-ride energy

The Waves

There are lake people. There are ocean people. In my experience, they are rarely one and the same.

I have navigated my way around some perspicuous lakes: Long Lake in Maine, Lake Como in

Italy, Blue Mountain Lake in the Adirondacks, the Wannsee in Berlin. Picturesque and pristine, alluring in a languid sort of way, a lake is where I go when I want to take a nap.

The rest of the time I go to the ocean. Because in the ocean I get to feel the waves.

When I visit Los Angeles, I stay in the North End of Manhattan Beach. Surf central. Watch the surfers descend from Highland Avenue to the ocean, wet-suit clad, boards tightly tucked under one arm. They hover like a flotilla of human iguanas in the Pacific, patiently waiting to ride the perfect wave. I love to watch the surfers do their thing. When I charge the waves, however, I prefer to bodysurf.

The ocean is an impetuous place. Waves can be shy; they can be ferocious. No wave is ever entirely like the next. Bigger is better in bodysurfing, just as it is in surfboarding, but there is no such thing as a perfect wave. There is only the wave, and the ideal moment in which to catch it as it ascends, right before it crests. That is when I thrust my arms forward and out, flatten my torso, lunge and submerge.

Think of bodysurfing as your perfect energy four-pack. Whenever we contemplate different forms of energy, we think first and foremost of four varieties: mental, emotional, physical, spiritual. In the act of bodysurfing, we access all four of these energy streams. We watch the waves as they roll toward us, pick the one we want to ride. Split-second decision. We experience an exuberant sense of excitement as we submerge into the wave. And every muscle in our body is wholly engaged.

The spiritual part? I think of the ocean as the soul of the world's ecosystem. Water is our connection to the source—raw, playful, invigorating, at times wild, at times serene. Each time we wade into the ocean, we encounter this energy. No matter how you experience spirit or spirituality, this energy is palpable.

Full energy absorption. That is the gift of the bodysurfing experience.

And the waves just keep coming.

Two Steps to Create Momentum

Let's leave the ocean for a moment.

Every moment of every day, energy waves roll toward us. Some are inner waves, some are outer waves. We either catch these energy waves or we don't. Our ability to ride an energy wave exponentially defines the quality of every moment that follows.

A thought is mental energy. When a thought persists, it becomes an inner wave. It may be activated by external stimulation, such as reading an article that stirs my thought. It may be activated by a link to my subconscious, as when my thought pops up as if out nowhere, and I often don't know why. I can choose to ride this thought wave, or I can direct my attention elsewhere.

If you're an obsessive thinker, your mental waves just keep coming. A thought grabs a hold of your mind and rolls on and on and on and on. It's as if you are bodysurfing a wave that never reaches shore. Your limbs get weary, your muscles ache, and you simply cannot disentangle from the wave.

Energy Armageddon.

Worse yet, because our mental energy tends to be so dominant, it often inhibits our ability to note other forms of energy. Emotion is our feeling reaction to people and situations, based on our moral compass and timeless experiences of loss, hurt, desire. Emotion is a form of energy that moves through the body, sometimes quickly, sometimes more slowly, much like a wave. When our thoughts become obsessive, we attach powerful emotions to these thoughts. We get stuck in one emotional state, and emotions start to fester. They no longer move through us like waves. Energy gets blocked.

Obsessive thought often renders us oblivious to our physical needs as well. We neglect to recharge our body with proper energy fuel. We do not provide it with the rest and recuperation time it requires. And we cut ourselves off from the spiritual energy that is all around us. Spiritual energy, in its purest form, is the energy that connects our soul to the spirit of people, places, things. We look at an ancient temple, and instead of just seeing an old stone structure, we sense the sacred energy that emanates from the building. We look at an old oak tree, and we sense the root energy of the tree. We see the smile of a stranger, and we sense the love and kindness that emanates from that stranger.

There are two steps to wave riding. They are simple. Notice the wave. And choose to ride it.

This is our reward. The second we catch an energy wave, we create momentum. Momentum is our conscious experience of forward motion. Forward motion infuses every moment that follows. Two steps. That's all it takes.

Momentum is a great thrill in the act of bodysurfing. It is just as invigorating in all other aspects of our life. How often have you left a conversation with someone and felt *energized by* the conversation? Allow me to translate: I was mentally stimulated. I was roused by the thoughts and ideas. I was stirred deep down in my soul. I wanted to get up and make the world a better place.

You experienced momentum.

There's only one way to get it. You gotta notice the energy cues.

How to Be a Pick-Up Artist

Word Story is a simple social game. Gather a group of 8, 10, 12 folks. Sit in a circle. Create a story together. You make it up as you go along, one word at a time. A person says a word. The person on either side adds another word. The person next to them adds another word. And so it goes.

A few rules: The sentences in the story, absurd though the story may turn out to be, must be grammatically correct. When it's your turn, you may say "comma" or "period" in lieu of adding a word. That's it. The story ends whenever it ends. And when it's your turn, you gotta jump in. Fast.

Word Story is a singular exercise in creating momentum and discovering meaning as you go along. Mental energy, emotional energy, creative energy, collective energy: There is lots of energy at play. The drill is split-second cuing. When the story comes your way, you have just seconds to add a word. One word. Words get jumbled in your head. Adrenaline pulses through your body. You do a gut-level possibility check. Then you have to spit it out. Your word.

A group of folks who surrenders to Word Story embarks on a rollicking energy ride. As a rehearsal for being fully engaged in a moment, Word Story is as good as it gets.

When I think of how we play the momentum game in our daily life, I think of two types of folks, the Let-Me-Think-About-It People and the Pick-Up Artists.

Let-Me-Think-About-It People face an impulse, an unexpected stimulus, a new piece of information with the instinct to step back. Reflect on the new information. Dissect the risks involved in getting on the ride. Gather a little bit of data. Mull it over. They eventually catch a wave. It rarely is the one that's right in front of them.

Sometimes, of course, the next wave doesn't come.

Pick-Up Artists tune into external stimulation quickly. They pick up the nuances of a language cue. They enjoy the back-and-forth of verbal banter. They are in tune with their internal prompts—thoughts, emotions, physical energy. They pick up on nonverbal cues as well. Sense the underlying mood, spirit, energy of a room the moment they walk through the door. Stepping back is rarely their first impulse. Pick-Up Artists prefer to step in. Quickly.

I value the benefits of considered reflection. It is an essential life skill that fosters substantive insight. I value it especially when the social stakes are high. But I also know that Pick-Up Artists are a lot more likely to experience the joy of momentum. They, in turn, create the joy of momentum for others. They fashion the more momentous life.

the moment

In my work as an executive coach, I support exceptional business leaders. Smart, driven go-getters. Brilliant strategic thinkers who are three steps ahead in every conversation they're in. Whenever I help one of these leaders to get ready for a high-stakes event, I often hear these words: "I didn't have enough time to prepare."

They're right. They really didn't have enough time to prepare. I can think of moments in my own life when I wished I had more time to prepare. Then I remember Word Story. In Word Story, our entire life up to this moment has been our preparation. Our mental agility, our instincts, our ability to energize ourselves—that's our preparation. Our willingness to let go of control. That's preparation. Our faith in prajna. Preparation.

"The reason they pay me the big bucks," my friend Tony San Marino, senior vice president of a venerable advertising agency in Manhattan, says to me, "is because my instincts have been well-honed over time. They trust my instincts."

Yes, a clear strategy can be beneficial in business and life. Planning fosters purposeful execution. But life in the moment is a cue game. A cue is a concrete and immediate signal through which energy communicates with us.

Notice. Respond. That's how momentum is created.

We create momentum when we move physically closer to another person.

We create momentum when we extend an extravagant gesture. A touch. A kiss.

We create momentum when we raise our voice, lower our voice.

We create momentum when we perform a disruptive act.

We create momentum when we smile.

Everything we do is a cue for the next moment.

It either creates or kills momentum.

"Until one is committed," the Scottish explorer W. H. Murray wrote, "there is hesitancy, the chance to draw back. Concerning all acts of initiative, there is one elementary truth that ignorance of which kills countless ideas and splendid plans: that the moment one definitely commits oneself, then providence moves too."[1]

Not prepare more and more and then some more. No. Commit.

Commitment will tempt us to ignore the cue that doesn't fit our plan. Go ahead, have your plan. But conscientiously engage with the cues that are coming your way.

Commit in the moment, to the moment. Commit split-second, cue by cue.

Providence will take care of the rest.

Momentum is the reward.

Shakti Comes for a Visit

There's energy, and there's what I call "big energy."

Be greedy with me for a moment. Let us contemplate the experience of big energy. Hindus call it *Shakti* or *prana*. The Chinese call it *chi*. The Japanese call it *ki*. I will use these words interchangeably for the remainder of this book. There are nearly a hundred different phrases around the world to describe this big energy. The most common English equivalent is the term "life-force." Sounds odd, doesn't it? "Life-force" is not a phrase we ever use. And most of us don't know what the heck this life-force is.

If you've ever had an acupuncture session with a skilled acupuncturist, you got a hit of Shakti. Acupuncture needles release chi and send it via energy pathways to specific organs in your body. The chi is precise. It has direction. It is palpable. You feel it. It is undeniable.

Powerful stuff.

Here is a moment of Shakti. I sit on a bench overlooking a cornfield in a remote rural area of Germany, about an hour and a half north of Frankfurt. I am alone on this bench. A country chapel hovers on a hilltop behind me. Wooden lookout towers line the perimeters of the cornfields and provide sweeping views of the valley. The field slopes down toward the small village of Thalheim, a village that doesn't figure on any tourist map of Germany. A smattering of houses. A country cemetery. A small bridge that crosses a brook. No stores, no restaurants, not even the ubiquitous German news kiosk. An utterly unremarkable place.

Have you ever stood directly under a waterfall? A tall one with a very long drop, where water thunders down on you from high above? The stream of water pummels your head and your shoulders with savage intensity. It feels like the force of the water is bruising your forehead, battering your skin, without ever letting up. Part of you thinks that you simply will not withstand this onslaught of water, and yet you don't want it to end. That is what Shakti on my German cornfield bench feels like.

My feet are firmly planted on the ground, my back presses into the back of the bench, and then light starts to pour down from the sky. White-golden light. It pours with the insistence of a waterfall, enters my body through the top of my forehead, through the shoulders. Shoots down my spine in the form of energy. Unlike the water that descends from a waterfall, this light washes directly into me. It pours and pours in undulating waves of intensity. As more light showers down, my entire body begins to quiver. I feel myself vibrating with the intensity of this light, a subtle but persistent vibration, as if I have just been plugged into one big cosmic energy socket.

This is the only requirement for going on a Shakti ride: Because you likely did not take a class on the essentials of big energy in high school or college, a sincere desire to know Shakti is a fine place to start. And the faith that a billion people all over the world who know the Shakti experience aren't all candidates for the mental ward.

There are three ways to activate Shakti. If you are fortunate, you may be blessed with a spontaneous Shakti awakening. My experience on the bench overlooking Thalheim was such a spontaneous gift—exquisite when it happens, hard to replicate. This gift is most likely to manifest during times of high personal duress or extreme relaxation. Being in physical proximity of an enlightened being with great Shakti energy may facilitate an awakening. But we cannot will it to happen.

If you don't wish to leave your Shakti experience up to chance, find a spiritual community that practices the ritual of *Shaktipat*. Shaktipat is a formal initiation in which a spiritual leader awakens your Shakti. Most commonly, however, Shakti channels are activated through our commitment to a specific personal energy practice. Yoga, chakra meditation, visualization, conscious breathing, chanting, tai chi, and qi gong are classic practices that release Shakti flow. These practices are not as dramatic as a spontaneous hillside Shakti shower. They open the Shakti doors slowly, gently, over time. But they get you to the hilltop.

Why does this matter? In my own life, connecting with chi was a game changer. The moment I began to more acutely experience energy in my body, I began to more acutely receive the energy that was all around me, the energy of people, places, things. It had been there all along, of course, but now my energy channels were open. Moment by moment, my life became energized.

In Praise of Body Signals

On a bright May morning in Manhattan, I grab a cappuccino with Blair Glaser, a licensed psychotherapist, mentor, and expert on professional authority. As we sit down in the coffee shop of the Andaz Hotel, across from the magnificent Main Public Library on Fifth Avenue, I immediately sense that Blair and I are kindred spirits. Not only do we share a multitude of professional interests, we both also received formal Shaktipat initiations in the same spiritual community. "Shaktipat," Blair explains, "has given me a dual awareness. There is the experience of a part of myself that is never changing. And then there is the part of me that is going through my everyday trials, tribulations, has doubts and fears." As sweet as a private Shakti moment is, I am really most interested in how our experience of big energy filters into how we experience a simple, ordinary moment.

"How do you experience energy between people?" I ask Blair.

"Body awareness is the key discipline," Blair says emphatically. "As I engage with a person, I pay attention to how I feel in the moment. I notice how the other person is reacting to me. I notice when my stomach gets tight. I notice when my shoulders scrunch up. And I pay attention to how I feel after I have been with a person. Am I drained or do I feel energized?"

And as if to make sure I don't miss the point, Blair adds: "This is something I have consciously worked on."

It is a treat to discuss energy dynamics with an energy-savvy thinker like Blair. Conventional psychological theory continues to perpetuate the "energy lite" version of energy. If you work in the corporate world, you have likely taken a battery of psychological assessments that define the parameters of your personality for you. You have been told that some folks are introverts who draw energy primarily from thought, reflection, reading, quiet time. You have been told that there are extroverts who primarily draw energy from engaging with other folks. The notion of big energy, commonplace in the majority of non-Western cultures, does not factor into this psychological paradigm. Neither does a conversation about body energetics.

Shakti doesn't care about your psychological profile. It is bigger than any psychological labels that have been assigned to you. It is available to introverts and extroverts. Shakti will show up in the blazing form of an energy shower from heaven. It will show up in the tiny energetic response we have in the middle of a conversation.

"For me," Blair Glaser explains, "energy is always a tangible sensation that I experience in my body. The moment we notice an energy signal, we are more consciously present in that moment. This awareness, in turn, leads us to act more authentically in any situation."

Go and have fun with your private Shakti practice. But beware. More energy signals will suddenly pop up within your body. More energy will stream toward you from the world outside.

The waves will start to roll.

The Aha Moment

On a visit to Pnom Penh, circa 2004, an 86-year-old Cambodian woman grabs the hand of Scott Neeson, the president of Sony Pictures. She leads Neeson to a garbage heap where he finds three young children, gravely ill with typhoid. In that instant, as Neeson approaches the three children, his cell phone rings. A well-known Hollywood actor is on the other end, complaining to Neeson that his private jet doesn't have the proper amenities on board.

"My life wasn't meant to be this difficult," the actor states with a sense of exasperation.[2]

That is the day Neeson decides to give up his job at Sony and commit himself fully to his charity work as the head of the Cambodian Children's Fund.

Neeson had a classic aha moment.

An aha moment impels personal insight. When we act on this insight, we unleash mega momentum. In Neeson's case, it singlehandedly changed the direction of his life. And an aha moment is rarely just a lucky accident. Neeson's aha didn't happen in his mansion in the Hollywood Hills. It didn't happen in the lobby of a five-star hotel in Pnom Penh. An aha moment shows up when we court a sense of creative dislocation. We trigger this dislocation the second we abandon the familiar and encounter the foreign.

When the tension between that which we know well and that which seems foreign becomes unbearable, when we can no longer reconcile our experience of the familiar with our experience of the foreign, circumstances scream for a mental shift. Aha.

Mental shifts change our lives.

So what are we gonna do? Hop on a plane and travel to the far reaches of the world?

Not so fast. Travel is a formidable way to kick up some energy dust. In a world in which we can access absolutely everything on the internet, however, a true encounter with the foreign is harder and harder to come by. You may find yourself walking the streets of Paris, Buenos Aires, Shanghai, Beirut. You may inhale a whiff of the exotic during your walk but are instantly comforted by the sight of every luxury brand you know from your shopping mall back home. When you disembark from your cruise ship, you stay with your tribe of fellow cruise-ship travelers. Your tour guide whisks you away on a sanitized culture tour. You spend the bulk of your time shopping for trinkets.

A faint whiff. No dislocation.

I am a well-traveled soul. My most life-altering aha, however, occurred close to home. It made me realize the foreign need not be a foreign country.

When the Foreign Is Within

Toward the end of a workaholic career as a theater director, I take 6 weeks off. When you're a workaholic, 6 weeks is an eternity. I book myself into a funky (and no longer existing) retreat center in Rimrock, Arizona—the Golden Phoenix. The Golden Phoenix is run by Reverend Mona, a pixieish woman in her early 50s who looks like she has seen better days.

The Phoenix is housed in an abandoned dude ranch that sits atop an ancient Anasazi burial mound. Ten of us live on this mound. We have time to ponder the beauty of the desert. We partake in early morning jump meditations to activate chi. Our bodies undergo a rigorous 3-week body detox. The crowning point of a stay at the Golden Phoenix is what Mona calls "The Intensive": 4 days of mental processing, self-awareness exercises. Mona calls it the "stop-the-bullshit" work. For someone like me, who has never really paused to look at himself, this is scary as hell.

On the third morning of The Intensive, all activity comes to a sudden halt. Reverend Mona stands in front of the group. She stares at the 10 of us with a sustained dramatic pause. She holds the pause, and then she announces, in a voice filled with withering disdain: "You are the most stubborn group of people I have ever met!"

Thus my descent into the foreign begins.[3]

This is the game. Mona tells me to lie on my bed, alone in my room, for several days and nights, an unspecified amount of time. I don't know how long because Mona won't say. My eyes will be blindfolded, my room shuttered dark. When I raise my hand, Mona or one of the other staff members will come and take me to the bathroom. When she taps me on the shoulder, she will bring food or drink.

The second I slip on my blindfold, I enter my dark night of the soul. Mona has shut every emergency exit. My physical world has shrunk to the narrow borders of this cot. I lie in silence, but it is an outer silence only. My skin feels like it is crawling with critters. On my skin, under my skin, inside my organs.

I have many visions that night. They come right after I enter the darkness. Sometimes life is a cliché. This is one of those moments. The night is the operator. It pushes the button, and in my mind a screen appears. Literally so. The film rolls. There is nothing I can do to stop it. No off switch, no brake. Memory has a very specific location that night, it sits right there on the screen in my forehead and unfurls with relentless alacrity. Moments chase other moments as if there isn't enough time to see them all. I am on that screen, am in every frame, but my eyes stand outside and watch. I become a witness in a race to my past. Every person I have known, every person I have loved, every person who has loved me, every person I have betrayed, every person I have abandoned.

When the film comes to an end—and it does, I don't know how many minutes, hours later—I turn into my bed and curl in. It feels like a collapse, yet I have collapsed before, and no collapse has ever felt like this; and how could I collapse where there is nothing to collapse into, but that is exactly what it feels like. I fold into the sheet on which I lie, every part of my body folds into it, folds and drops down, my arms clutch the other sheet that covers me, pulls it tight, and then my bed becomes the ocean where I drown.

"You looked so still on your cot," Mona says to me two and a half days later as she pulls off my blindfold. "Like you had died."

I have two aha moments during my dark night of the soul.

A voice whispers: *Write. Write.* Repeatedly. Insistently.

And I see a little white house on a cliff, surrounded by lush tropical vegetation, overlooking the sea. The little white house keeps appearing, again and again. I know instinctively that my white house isn't a metaphor. It is an actual white house, somewhere on some island.

I know I have to find it.

I never figured out what kind of reverend Mona was. But I realize now that she took me on her version of a vision quest, one of the traditional rites of passage in many Native American cultures. In a vision quest, a person leaves the familiar world to spend a period of days and nights in nature. This time is spent in complete isolation, with the explicit intent of gaining spiritual guidance.

The foreign goes deep. I was in a dusty part of Arizona where I had never been before. Foreign. I was with 10 people who I had not previously met. I lived on top of a Native American burial mound, a place filled with spirit energy. My body experienced radical detoxification.

And the ultimate foreignness, of course: Myself.

Six months after my visit to the Golden Phoenix, I move into a little white house in Tobago, on a cliff overlooking the Atlantic Ocean.

And I begin to write.

The Foreign in Your Backyard

"The foreign can often be found right around the corner," Blair Glaser suggests.

So true. Blair and I talk about the experience of seeing a therapist, the formal protocol of this very peculiar encounter between two people—usually seated, facing each other, clearly defined roles. A social exchange where the focus is squarely on one person, with the explicit purpose of eliciting an aha moment for that individual. Foreign, indeed.

Attend a church service or spiritual gathering by a community whose beliefs differ from yours.

Visit a social club where no one speaks your language.

Join a Meetup chapter where folks are passionate about a hobby you know nothing about.

Read a book you said you'd never read, watch a movie you said you'd never watch, go to a concert by a band whose music drives you bonkers.

Spend a day by yourself, without making plans with anyone, without a single electronic communication device at hand.

The foreign. Decide what that is for you. Go and walk into it.

You may experience an aha moment, you may not. You will most likely encounter some creative dislocation. Energy will be stirred, major energy. That is 100 percent guaranteed.

Come to think of it, why would you not do any of those things?

When We Surrender

"There is someone in the house."

Isabel Malone, a visitor in my little bungalow in Tobago, leans into the doorframe of my bedroom. I see Isabel's shadowy outline, hear her whispered voice. Moonlight spills through an open window into the room.

Then I scream.

I scream from the bottom of my groin, from the depths of my lungs, from the seat of my soul. My scream is ferocious. It shakes my entire body. I scream until my throat hurts, scream with a vehemence I did not know I possessed.

The scream has come out of nowhere. I had no idea I had that kind of scream inside of me.

The shadow of a person jumps over the ledge of the veranda and vanishes into the garden. Isabel and I step onto the terrace. We pause for a moment and gaze at the moonlight as it shimmies on the dark cover of the Atlantic. Then we lock the doors.

The man, it turns out, was a harmless vagrant. That is Trini-speak for a homeless person.

I learned that night that even in my little village in Tobago, I need to lock my doors and windows.

And I learned that when I don't have time to think, I can scream.

On the morning of August 20, 2013, a troubled young man charges through the doors of the McNair Learning Discovery Center and embarks on a shooting rampage. Michael Brandon Hill has not taken his medication for a mental disability. He has an AK-47 assault rifle on him and 500 rounds of ammunition. Antoinette Tuff, the school's bookkeeper, is alone in the main office of this suburban Atlanta elementary school. It is a day when she isn't supposed to work.

"This is not a joke," Hill shouts at Tuff. "I need you to understand this is not a joke. I am here. This is real. We are all going to die today."

As Hill props open one of the school's doors and starts to randomly shoot at the police officers that have now surrounded the school, Tuff is certain that Hill is about to be killed by a police bullet. She beckons him to return to the office and stay with her. With a 911 operator on the telephone and the shooter in her room, Tuff embarks on a fly-by-the-seat-of-her-pants conversation with the shooter that leads him to eventually surrender himself. Tuff tells Hill that she had thought of committing suicide after her husband of 26 years left her. Mentions her adult son who has multiple disabilities. Makes it clear that her life hasn't been a bed of roses. She reassures Hill that she loves him and that everything will be okay. Tuff stays calm. Her tone is resolute and empathetic.

"I was so scared," Tuff tells the 911 operator the second Hill is subdued.

Antoinette Tuff's conversation with Michael Brandon Hill prevents the sort of massacre that a year earlier killed 20 children and adults in an elementary school in Newtown, Connecticut. Tuff spent 15 minutes alone in a room with a man who might have been her killer. She is instantly hailed a hero. What forces come into play, I wonder, in the heroic act? What drives us when there is no time to think, no time to plan, and all we can do is respond?

Tuff, a devout Christian, knows her answer to that question.

> "I know today," Tuff tells CNN's Anderson Cooper, "that all I went through was actually for that one perfect day, and that was to save this one young man's life, and to make sure 800-and-some children and also all our staff would be able to know that God is real."[4]

Tuff surrendered to her God energy. Call it what you will. Higher Power. Primal instinct. Divine Guidance. This is the central gift of the heroic moment: We abandon any pretense of being prepared. We relinquish any illusion of being in control. We simply ride the wave. And we learn what stuff we are made of.

How sweet that is.

Everyday Heroics

You and I have the opportunity to create our own heroic moment, every single day. Not by tussling with an AK-47 shooter, I hope. No, we do it one surrender at a time.

As I chat with the effortlessly articulate Meredith Porte, she describes a specific moment of surrender for me. Meredith is a seasoned journalist who for many years hosted her own television program on WLRN Public Television in Miami. Her expansive spirit is, I have no doubt, fueled by decades of studying and teaching meditation with a global spiritual organization, the Brahma Kumaris.

"A lot of special things have happened in my life," Meredith asserts, "when other people couldn't do something."

Then Meredith and I dissect her moment of surrender. Like most acts of surrender in our daily lives, it involves a series of conscious shifts.

Meredith is invited to host a panel event at the University of Miami about balancing mind, body, and spirit. Meredith is passionate about this topic, and she has a good deal of experience in hosting such events. But the invitation to host comes at the last minute because the original host is unexpectedly unavailable. Meredith's first reaction is to say no. "I like to prepare, and there simply wasn't enough time to do so," she explains. "So I told myself, *I can't do this; this is not the right time.*"

Meredith quickly shifts this initial response. "I just assure myself that this is an opportunity. I am, after all, one of the organizers of the event. And I decide that when I am there it will be simply a matter of feeling the experience."

And Meredith prepares, anyway.

An hour before the start of the event, Meredith gathers backstage with her three panelists. Each of them has ideas about what topics to address and which areas of conversation might best be avoided. As Meredith listens, she quickly realizes that all of her preparation is for naught.

"I had to give it up," Meredith declares. "I had to go into the experience and surrender."

Another conscious shift. And then Meredith chronicles her final act of surrender.

"I walk out and I see the audience. The room is fully packed with about 250 people. Their energy is amazing, so I decide to meditate and send energy back to the room. I do this with my eyes open. We are so limited by our thoughts and our words. I simply remind myself that I am energy and I am light. This helps me get into a state where what is happening is not about you and me. I consider this the state of soul consciousness. When I get to that state, I am able to allow things to unfold. And I can trust that everything that needs to be said will be said."

An exquisite description of our basic energy two-step: Notice the wave. And choose to ride it.

It really is that simple. Our first impulse often is, as Meredith so astutely observes, to dismiss the energy of a moment.

Don't dismiss energy. Notice it. Notice energy in all of its forms—the mental, the emotional, the physical kind. Notice the spirit energy. Notice the Shakti. The body signals. Your soul consciousness.

Surrender is not a caving in. It is a mental shift. It is the insight that, in this moment, it will be more helpful to not force action. It is the trust that this moment will take care of itself better than anything that I may foist upon it.

Meredith's panel event was a fine success. But you knew that, didn't you?

Explorations for Key #3: Wave-Ride Energy

When we begin to notice energy in its many different forms, the opportunities for wave-riding are endless. We suddenly see a chance to give energy, receive energy, join energy at every turn. Whenever people tell us to seize the moment, what they really mean is seize the energy of the moment. When we do, we are blessed with the gift of momentum.

To help you optimize your wave-riding experience, have some fun with the following explorations. Each of them will crystallize your experience of energy.

Conduct Energy Check-Ins

An energy check-in is a fine way to stay conscious of what is happening inside of you at any given time during the day. It's quick. It's an internal act, so you can do it anywhere, anytime. Over dinner with family. In the middle of a business meeting. In a moment of solitude, as you ride the subway or drive your car.

Here's how it goes. Think of our energy four-pack: mental, emotional, physical, spiritual energy. Do a silent four-pack energy scan.

How is my mental energy? Is my mind calm? Is it focused, is it agitated, is it obsessed? Is it at peace?

What am I feeling? Joyous, anxious, sad, nervous, excited? Nothing, perhaps? Calm?

How is my physical energy? Charged, tired, tight, relaxed?

And how is my spirit right now? Hopeful, dejected, isolated, connected?

The purpose of a check-in is not to fix anything. Notice your energy. Accept where it is, in that moment. And if you feel the need to create an energetic shift for yourself, you will know where to begin.

Conduct an energy check-in spontaneously, anytime. If you are a goal-oriented person, you may wish to set yourself a daily goal. Three times a day, once every hour. You decide.

This will be your reward: Over time, you create a keen sensitivity to your own energy signals. As you notice more of your own signals, you will also better note the energy signals around you. You will be riding a lot more waves.

Get a Chi Experience

The moment we get a personal taste of big energy, the world around us seems to sizzle with more energy everywhere. It was simmering with this energy all along, of course—but now that our chi is released, we more readily connect with the chi that is all around.

Some key chi-activators: yoga, reflexology, tai chi, qi gong, acupuncture, Reiki, chakra meditation.

Some of these practices, such as acupuncture, Reiki, and reflexology, are passive. We receive the gift of chi through the work of an expert chi practitioner. Some practices, such as yoga, tai chi, and qi gong, are active and involve the performance of active ritualized movement on our part. The specific movement practices activate our chi.

All of these practices add vitality to your life. They energize you. They just plain feel good. I cannot think of a single reason to not have a little fun with them—even if they take you into the experience of the foreign.

If you do not know where to begin, start with yoga. If you already enjoy yoga, add another chi practice. Yoga classes are readily available anywhere these days, and the benefits of yoga easily extend to a practice we'll spend a little more time on in Key #4—meditation.

Choose Behaviors that Foster Momentum

Momentum is the delicious experience of forward motion. It propels us into new experiences, invites fresh insights, and adds a sense of discovery and adventure to our lives. Two specific sets of behavior explicitly foster momentum. Experiment intentionally with these behaviors.

Pick Up Your Cues

There are events and circumstances that benefit from careful reflection before we respond. Many simple everyday situations, however, unfold more gracefully when we notice a cue and respond.

Note the many different forms of cues that come your way. A verbal cue. A physical gesture. A wave of emotion. An idea. Prajna is a cue that comes to you from within. When you respond to a cue quickly, you add energy to that cue. When you don't, the energy will dissipate or be expressed in another form.

A caution about picking up emotional cues: When I pick up the joy of another person, I help magnify the joy. When I pick up the anger of another person, I magnify that as well. When it comes to emotional waves, beware of the waves you ride and the waves you choose to pass up.

Explore the Foreign

Because an encounter with the foreign is a singular way of creating personal momentum, create opportunities to meet "your foreign." You decide what that is for you. If this involves traveling to a faraway country, leave familiar trappings behind and fully submit to the foreign experience. A simple way to meet your foreign is to find it in your own backyard. You may wish to begin with some of the options mentioned in this chapter. Better yet, get clear on what would constitute a truly foreign experience for you.

The moment you step into a "momentum mindset," opportunities for quickly picking up cues and meeting the foreign will show up everywhere.

If you are a goal-oriented person, consider setting simple goals: One intentional visit a month to a foreign place in your own backyard, one hour a day where you engage in whatever it is you're doing and stay mindful of picking up your cues.

And never forget that these are meant to be joyful explorations, not chores!

key
number
four

key #4:

make time stand still

The Silence

Speed and stillness. Silence and noise.

Ostensible opposites. Our ability to fully experience the paradox, this contrast between seemingly incongruous states of being, is the special sauce that helps us savor every aspect of life. One state informs the other. Palate enriched.

Sounds simple, doesn't it? The rush-rush of our increasingly distracted lives, however, eradicates the experience of contrast. We have minds that rush-rush and never rest. We have bodies that push-push until we fold with exhaustion. We have emotions that run rampant and hold us hostage. We daily ride the wave that never reaches shore.

Slowing down and settling into a moment of stillness is the thing many of us desire most. It is also the thing we go to inordinate lengths to avoid. I think of a classic song of the hippie era, Simon and Garfunkel's "The Sound of Silence."[1] When we finally get still, we begin to hear the sound of silence. It isn't always celestial. It is more often a ceaseless rehashing of our mental obsessions. Gruff, unrelenting. As the chatter subsides, we also hear the occasional sound of wisdom. The whisper of the divine.

And we know a little bit of peace.

In my first year after college, I am hired to be a performer for a children's theater company. That is as truly unglamorous as it sounds: 9 months of trekking in a minibus to elementary schools in the larger Washington DC area, performing on sad little stages, for audiences that will scream at anything.

And there is a paradox. For 2 weeks around Christmas time, we set up shop in the very grown-up Terrace Theater at the Kennedy Center for the Performing Arts, perform a holiday show commissioned by the Center. We have ample dressing rooms. We're greeted with respect at the stage door. Yes, contrast.

I play a character called "the Silence." Four actors portray members of a family that is embroiled in the sort of petty daily squabbles we all know too well. These squabbles reach new heights under the pressures of the holiday season. Whenever a quarrel gets too out of hand, the Silence enters the room. With the arrival of Silence, the blather slowly fades away. A hush settles over the family. A temporary sense of serenity fills the house.

As the show reaches its final moments, the family learns to appreciate the simpler gifts of the holiday season. It settles into moments of quiet contemplation. Joy without distraction. A tenuous connection to the divine.

It experiences the Silence.

I don't enjoy playing this character, at all. I am envious of my fellow actors who get to deliver all the juicy lines. They are given full reign to argue and shout and be dramatic. I don't have a single line of dialogue. All I get to do is, well, be silent.

I have, of course, the best part.

Silence wants to drop in for a visit, all the time. It wants to shower us with its gifts. Let us take a peek at what happens when we open the door and let it in.

Into Stillness

Take Exit 17 on Interstate 110, just a few miles south of downtown Los Angeles, head east toward the Long Beach Freeway, and you will soon stumble upon the city of Huntington Park. It is one of the many unheralded gateway communities in the Greater Los Angeles area. Huntington Park does not register on any tourist map of Southern California. It is resolutely ordinary, largely forgotten. Aspire Ollin Preparatory Academy is a charter school in this small working-class community. Its students, grades 7 through 9, look crisp in their blue-and-grey school uniforms, gleaming white shirts topped at the collar with a black tie. They study the subjects we would expect—Math, English, Spanish, American History, Physical Education.

And for 20 minutes, twice a day, they practice Transcendental Meditation.

Quiet Time, the school's meditation program, is sponsored by the David Lynch Foundation to help create schools where all students meditate. The actress Judy Greer captures the impact of this program at Aspire Ollin in an exquisite 7-minute film short.[2]

I am stirred by the resolve of the school's principal, Jennifer Garcia. She understands that a ritual that calms the mind and reduces stress is as important as studying for the next exam.

"This tool is a life tool," Ms. Garcia asserts.

I am stirred by the testimonials from a group of young meditators. One by one, they affirm the sense of peace they feel when they quiet their minds. Victor, a shy young fellow with a cherubic face, beams as he talks about the gifts of meditation. "I am calm," Victor declares with a wide-open smile, "and I am not in a bad mood."

Victor had been the sort of young man who struggled with his emotions and hid in his room a lot. "Once meditation began," Victor's mother explains, "he started to get along with us. I see him more peaceful, more relaxed. I can see a lot of changes in him since he started meditating."

Frederick Tan didn't have the benefit of learning meditation in middle school. As Fred and I share a meal at Timpano Chophouse on Fort Lauderdale's Las Olas Boulevard, I am drawn to his genial presence and his relaxed yet formal demeanor. Fred's life straddles two seemingly disparate worlds. He is a senior wealth director for one of the world's foremost wealth management firms. Fred is also a meditation teacher and the coowner of Daily Offering Yoga Studio in Miami's MiMo District, as well as the creator of Paraveda, an online guided meditation program.

"Meditation showed up in my life when I was working on Wall Street," Fred explains. "I found myself dealing with a level of stress I had not experienced before. I was getting overly anxious. I tried lifting weights and jogging but found that these activities weren't relaxing me. I became even more of a tight bundle in my body."

Yoga turned out to be Fred's entry to meditation. Fred is an ardent advocate for the benefits of *pranayama*, specific yoga breathing exercises that release prana in our body. In my own life, I found my way into meditation through a Hindu community. In my practice, as in many Hindu practices, chanting leads into meditation. Transcendental Meditation, *Vipassana* meditation, Zen meditation, Yoga meditation, Hindu meditation, Loving Kindness meditation, Guided Meditation: There are nearly as many different forms of meditation as there are languages in the world.

"In yoga, we start with the physical," Fred elaborates. "That's what I love about it. Yoga leads me from the gross body to the subtle and occasionally the sublime. Breathing exercises reconnect me to the life-force of consciousness. Pranayama is the bridge between the body and the mind."

The Nuances of Breath

A focus on breath is the foundation of any meditation practice. From the mind, into the body. For Victor and his fellow meditators at Aspire Ollin, the silent repetition of a mantra goes hand-in-hand with their attention to breath. Eric Butterworth, one of the legendary metaphysical teachers of the late 20th century, taught me a very simple mantra that I cherish to this day. For more than 3 decades, Eric served as a Unity minister in Manhattan. Every Sunday morning, Eric and his wife, Olga, held a service at Lincoln Center's majestic Avery Fisher Hall. Eric championed a practical sort of mysticism. "As you inhale," Eric suggested, "say to yourself 'God is.' As you exhale, 'I am.'" *God is/I am. God is/I am. God is/I am.*[3]

Eric's mantra is identical to the well-known Sanskrit mantra *So hum* that first appeared in Sanskrit literature in the medieval period. "I am that. I am the force behind everything. I am one with the divine." While I repeat the mantra, my breath and the mantra quickly become one. I am breathing the mantra, the mantra breathes me. Its simple words carry an extraordinary energy. Prana activates.

"How do you personally experience bliss?" I ask Fred Tan. His answer goes to the heart and soul of why meditation is becoming an increasingly popular practice for folks all around the world.

"Bliss is peace," Fred replies without hesitation. "My meditation and my breathing get to the point where I become so relaxed that my breathing pattern alters. I am fully aware of being still, and I lose complete awareness of my body. My entire awareness rests in the cave of my heart. My mind forgets that it exists. This is my state of liberation. And I experience great peace."

Now that is worth meditating for.

One more paradox: You and I do not receive the gift of peace by going on a mission to chase the gift. Liberation becomes possible only as we detach from the distractions of the material world. This process of detachment during the act of meditation is called *vairagya*. It's a Sanskrit term that can be loosely translated as "letting go."[4] As we meditate, we move through three levels of letting go. With yoga and breath, we let go of tension in our body. In the second level of *vairagya*, we let go of the desires that may show up as we meditate—the urge to get up and grab a snack, the itch to suddenly clean the house. In the third level of *vairagya*, we let go of our identification with our thoughts. We notice our thoughts as they come and go. We watch them from a distance. That is the shift in our consciousness. Instead of being the thinker, we become the watcher of the thoughts.

When meditation takes us into a state of bliss, we may hear a voice that says "I don't ever want this feeling to end."

Then we let go of that voice as well.

When Work Becomes Meditation

A sense of calm. An evidence of peace.

Exquisite experiences in the private act of meditation. They invoke a state of being that some of us have forgotten and many of us have not previously known. How, then, do we carry the rewards of such private moments into our work and our public life?

Pico Iyer is the best-selling author of a dozen books including *The Art of Stillness: Adventures in Going Nowhere*. A globe-trotting storyteller, Iyer writes eloquently about the excesses of a consumerist world and the yearning to reconnect with our inner life.[5] Iyer turned his back on a high-octane Manhattan life and now resides with his family in a small village in Japan. He regularly retreats to a Benedictine monastery on the Central California coast. And he doesn't meditate.

Krista Tippett, host of the radio program *On Being*, inquires about this well-known fact.

"My wife wakes up every morning at 5:00 a.m. and meditates," Iyer chuckles, "and I lie in bed, watch her meditating, and then collapse in a heap. I do it vicariously through her."

And then, as he acknowledges that his friends constantly ask him why he doesn't meditate, Iyer elaborates.

"If my wife were here, she would laugh and say, 'Krista, all this guy ever does is meditate.' Just because I'm a writer. And so she sees me, I wake up, I have breakfast, I make a 5-foot commute to my desk, and then I just sit there for at least 5 hours trying to sift through my distortions and illusions and projections and find what is real behind the many things I'm tempted to say."[6]

If meditation is a conscious engagement with the present moment, then writing is, indeed, an act of meditation. So are a host of other activities. My friend Rob Doucet is an avid gardener. Rob lives in the quintessential South Florida home, an L-shaped structure that shelters a pool, luscious vegetation that wraps all around. Unlike some South Floridians, Rob does all of his own gardening. Rob enjoys envisioning the shape and scale of each nook of his garden. He loves to roam a nursery and handpick every single shrub and perennial that will go into the ground. He savors the moments when he gets to dig down into the dirt with his hands, feel the wet soil glide through his fingers. Relishes the textured sprawl of his foxtail ferns, the sweet heady smell of the pure white gardenias, the spotted trunk of his voodoo lilies.

Rob loves to garden.

"Gardening is an act of meditation for me," he explains.

Activity as a form of meditation: It seems relatively easy when our work is between us and our mind. Or when we handle objects such as plants. When we bake. When we clean a house, when we operate a machine in a factory. But how do we maintain a meditative calm when we engage with other humans? How do we carry a sense of stillness into our frequently turbulent places of work?

"In the financial world," Fred Tan suggests, "it is natural to lead with facts, analysis, statistics. What we think of as left-brain stuff. We can easily get lost in thought, and we lose track of the intention in our interactions. Regardless of the specific business purpose, the deeper purpose for me is always to establish connection."

We all know the experience of getting lost in thought. The moment when we speak up in a meeting and make an eloquent point, and then, of a sudden, we feel like we are talking into the void. How do we redirect ourselves?

"I do breathing exercises to bring myself back to my heart," Fred explains. "I reset myself. I do this to make sure my mind is not trying too hard to control. I reset to allow the conversation to flow more freely."

"What do you do when you are in the presence of someone who is not open to you?" I wonder. "How do you react when you sense hostility or resistance?"

"I work intentionally at opening myself up," Fred answers. "I work on my own resistance to the other person not being open. I open my heart up to this person. I consciously expand my breath to the heart. I breathe deeply into my heart chakra. The moment I do, there usually is some shift that I experience. Even if I just sit back and listen. I surrender and feel into it. Back to the heart."

And back to meditation basics. From the mind, into the body. How easy it is for us to forget. Yet this is one of the many beauties of the mindful life. When we forget, we get to catch ourselves. Again and again.

In the beginning, in the end, always breath.

Walking to the Airport

Will Self likes to walk. On a Saturday afternoon in November 2006, Self lands at JFK Airport in New York City and walks into Manhattan to attend a literary function on his behalf. A 20-mile journey. Self has earlier walked the entire 26 miles from his home in South London to Heathrow Airport to catch his flight to JFK.[7]

Will Self is the acclaimed British author of 10 satirical novels and a frequent commentator on BBC Radio 4. Self has turned the act of walking into a political statement. He has flown to Dubai and walked in the desert heat from Dubai International Airport to his hotel. He has landed at LAX and walked to downtown Los Angeles. In London, Self regularly walks from his neighborhood into the countryside outside the city. It takes him a good portion of a day before the first fields of the Lea Valley and the brush of Epping Forest come into view.

Yes, Will Self walks.

"People don't know where they are anymore," Self says. "In the postindustrial age, this is the only form of real exploration left. Anyone can go and see the Ituri Pygmy, but how many people have walked all the way from the airport to the city?"

Walking is a supreme act of slowing down. Mr. Self chooses to spend his first night in New York City at a Crowne Plaza Hotel near the airport. He discovers that leaving JFK Airport on foot is no small feat. To reach his hotel, Self ends up crossing multiple expressways in the dark of night, without the protection of a pedestrian walkway or lights.

The following morning, as Self embarks on his walk to Manhattan, he strolls past a dizzying display of holiday decorations in the middle-class neighborhood of South Ozone Park, passes blocks and blocks of housing projects in East New York and Brownsville, mom-and-pop auto-body shops, vacant lots enveloped by barbed wire and guarded by malevolent dogs, more churches than he had thought possible. For a while, Self is trailed by a mysterious black SUV. When he asks a passerby for directions, Self is met with disbelief. The notion of walking to Manhattan stretches the bounds of credulity with this stranger.

When Self finally catches his first glimpse of the Brooklyn Bridge, the majesty of the view compels him to hear a Gershwin score, heralding from the skies.

Arrived.

It is easy to dismiss Self's walk as the experiment of a man who has too much time on his hands. You and I will likely never make this walk. We will also never know the rich psychogeography of one of the great cities of the world.

Everyday Acts of Slowness

If you own a dog who needs to be walked, you already have a special relationship to the psychogeography of your neighborhood. You see the chinks and cracks in your sidewalks that drivers miss and ordinary pedestrians don't notice. You meet folks during your walks that you would otherwise never meet. You amble down alleys that you would normally avoid. At times, you surrender. You let your dog lead you.

Even when you feel rushed by the demands of a certain day, your dog walk does for you what you otherwise can't do for yourself. You slow down.

The benefits of slowing down are self-evident. All over the world, folks are starting to say no to our addiction to speed. Folks do so in every aspect of their lives. Parents who reject the notion of accelerated learning for their children have rediscovered the Rudolf Steiner schools.[8] Steiner frowned upon the idea that children should learn certain life skills before they are ready. Children need not learn how to read before they are 7 years old, Steiner affirmed. Instead, allow them to spend their early years telling stories, drawing, playing, and discovering nature.

Couples who are weary of their lets-get-it-over-with sex lives are discovering tantric sex. Think of it as the art of nonperformative sex. In a culture that values efficient performance in pretty much every aspect of life, shifting into an appreciation of nonperformance is a radical adjustment. Instead of racing toward a climax, tantric practices encourage the intentional delay of an orgasm. Both partners take their time with sensual touching, languid exploration, playful discovery. They reconnect with the experience of sex as a sacred act between two souls.

No matter in which part of your life you slow down, the benefit is always the same. A noticing. A savoring. An appreciation of the subtle. A willingness to be surprised by the ordinary. A richer settling into a moment.

I live 6 blocks from downtown Hollywood, just north of Miami. When I meet friends for dinner, I have been known to hop in the car and hunt for a parking space 6 blocks away. I now walk. It takes no longer than climbing into my car, starting the engine, opening the gate to the alley, pulling out of my property, closing the gate, turning into 20th Avenue and then, almost at once, beginning the quest for a spot to park.

My first impulse as I walk is to walk briskly. It requires a conscious commitment to slow myself into a leisurely stroll. My reward? With each 6-block walk, I notice a new facet of my neighborhood. A gardenia bush that shines differently in the early evening light. An elderly neighbor I have not seen before, peering out from behind a closed window. A fresh coat of pale green paint on the corner condo. The smell of barbecued steak wafting toward me from the recesses of a hidden courtyard. Without exerting any effort at all, my walk becomes a walking meditation. I am physically and mentally present, here in Hollywood, on this particular evening. I feel my breath and I sense my surroundings. I arrive at my destination calm, not harried.

I am learning. One walk at a time.

Unobligated Time

It seems like the impossible dream. To carve out unobligated time.

We complain that we don't have enough time to do all the things we wish to do. For many of us, it's a true statement. We truly don't have enough time. We ardently desire a "time-out" from our obligations.

Some call this time-out "me time." A faintly derogatory term, it smacks of self-indulgence, narcissism. I feel queasy when I hear these descriptors because I don't wish to be any of those things.

The moment I claim a slice of "me time," I instantly obligate this time. I get the spa treatment I have postponed for months, the facial that is overdue. I finally play squash with my buddy Raul, go to see the French movie with my friend Lori that she has raved about.

All cool things, I know. Still obligated time.

We're talking about something more radical here: a chunk of time for which you make absolutely no plans. Not a single one. Because you do not yet know what your state of mind will be come Saturday morning. What you will wish to do. What you may not wish to do.

Imagine.

You wake up in the morning. You may go for a run. You may not. You may drink a cup of coffee, you may not. You may read a book. You may not. You will eat not because it's time to eat but because you're hungry. You may lie in bed for 30 minutes and stare at the ceiling and do nothing. You may get in your car and drive nowhere in particular. You get to stop wherever you wish. You get to leave again whenever you want. Most important, you get to ignore the story of what you "should be doing with your time." The obligation story.

You get to listen to yourself.

It sounds improbable, I know. You have a family. Your children need you. Your spouse craves quality time with you. And you love your family and your children and your spouse. Your friends are itching to congregate with you, and you love them as well.

More story. More reasons to unobligate yourself.

Your Unobligate Experiment

Unobligate, just for a slither of time. A day, perhaps. Half a day. You decide. Schedule your unobligated time. A paradox, I know.

The folks you feel obligated to will be just fine.

Here's what unobligated time will do for you. You get to hear yourself. You get to say yes to your desires.

You get to ignore them. More imperatively, you get to notice every thought, impulse, hunch, craving, whim, body signal. You get to be real with yourself.

And you get to choose.

Moment by moment, you begin to liberate yourself from the tyranny of time. You unravel the story of what you should be doing with your time. You rediscover the freedom to be yourself.

It may feel a little uncomfortable.

If you have ever been to a silent retreat, you have had a glimpse of unobligated time. A silent retreat is usually organized by a specific spiritual group or community to facilitate your quiet contemplation. It does so by ensuring that your basic physical needs are met. The organizers may impose varying degrees of structure on how the quiet time is spent. Most important, a silent retreat removes your access to familiar distractions. You stop doing and more doing. The exit doors are closed. You get still.

A silent retreat is like running a prajna marathon. The insights keep coming and coming.

And yet, you are still in obligated time.

Unobligated time is the most radical personal choice you will make. You get to be silent if you so desire. You get to cook a brilliant meal for everyone you love. You get to create whatever you wish to create. You get to observe your desires. All exit doors are open. You get to play on a vast inner canvas. And you get to roam an infinite outer world.

Just for that slither of time, you get your choice back.

What you hear, what you act on, what you walk away from during unobligated time infiltrates everything that follows. Because when we get real with ourselves, we get real with others. Each subsequent moment is enriched.

Unobligated time is a magical playground in which we approach every second with the curiosity of a child and the wisdom of an adult.

And pardon me if this is obvious. Unobligated time feels pretty darn good.

Why not?

When Time Becomes Timeless

I used to think that when I have all the time in the world, time will no longer matter. Then I moved to Tobago. It was my year of relatively unobligated time. I had left one career and did not know what would come next. I was blessed with a minor reserve of money and did not need to work. I had lots of time on my hands.

I was still beholden to linear time.

Sitting on the terrace of my house, my feet propped onto the railing, under the shade of a spiraling mango tree, I flip through the pages of Graham Greene's *Our Man in Havana*. Then I hear a faint rumbling in the distance. The rumbling soon gets louder. A thunder and repeated thuds, approaching my house from the east. It's the public bus from Scarborough, hitting every pothole on the Old Road in Lambeau where I live, winding its way toward the airport on the western tip of the island. I know an hour has just passed.

Another rumble, an hour later. A gentle marker, yes. Still marking time.

You know the phrase "I lost track of time?" Well, you didn't actually lose track of time. You were in a state where time no longer mattered. You were involved in an experience that rendered our notion of time irrelevant. For a while.

There are two ways to reach this exalted state. We get there when we tend to our three levels of *vairagya*. Let go and let go and let go some more until peace comes for a visit, perhaps. As the sensation of peace seeps into our mind and settles in our bones, we stop marking time.

We also get there when we fully engage in an activity that matters to us. I love the novels of Graham Greene. All of them. They transport me to a world of foreign intrigue and subterfuge and a sense of cultural dislocation that I find both disconcerting and exhilarating. When I am fully absorbed in the act of reading a book that thrills me, I no longer hear the rumbling of the bus. My attention does not go to the pinch of my sciatica or the gurgling sound in the water pipes of my house. I find myself instead in the backstreets of Havana or the foothills of Haiti with Mr. Greene. I am transported.

Your Absorption Reward Card

Think of a time when you were fully absorbed in an activity that thrilled you. If you're a craftsman, you were perhaps building the perfectly proportioned table. If you're a marketing strategist, you were creating an ad campaign that turned your industry upside down. If you're a tennis player, you were hitting balls with a friend who is just a tad more skilled than you and challenged you to raise your game.

When you stop and look at a clock, you're astounded. Whew. Time flew by. What you thought had lasted mere minutes has actually taken hours.

The magic of full absorption.

When I am absorbed, I am not separate from the task I am performing. My mind is fully alert. My thoughts are not aimlessly ruled by the desires of my subconscious. They act in full support of the task at hand. My emotions are in sync with my engagement in the activity. My soul is nourished by the activity I am performing. All of my attention is focused on the task at hand.

Mihaly Csikszentmihalyi, our foremost authority on the psychology of optimal experience, calls this experience "flow."[9] When we're in flow, we deeply enjoy the activity we're performing. And there are some surprising factors that facilitate this state of flow. Flow doesn't happen when we coast. If an activity is too easy for us, we are likely to get bored. If it is too challenging, we are likely to get frustrated. Flow happens when there is a perfect balance between challenge and skills.

In many of our routine daily activities, we perform a task and our mind wanders off to contemplate extraneous matters—what we plan to have for dinner that evening, what the weekend holds in store. When we are in flow, action and mental awareness are fully aligned. Because of this alignment, we do not worry about failure. Our mind is squarely focused on the purposeful execution of our task. Thanks to this singular focus, any sense of self-consciousness falls away as well. We are not worried about what other people think of us. We are not concerned about how we "come across." We are absorbed.

As we fully experience a sense of flow during an activity, Csikszentmihalyi points out, this activity becomes autotelic for us. Autotelic activity is any act we perform as an end in and of itself. We gain satisfaction purely through our performance of this act. Extrinsic motivation is not required.

Let's be clear. When you lie on the beach and do absolutely nothing, it may indeed be an autotelic experience for you. It may be something you rather enjoy, for a while. It will not invoke an experience of flow, however. Chances are, you will get a little restless. You will soon be checking your clock. If it is a breezy sort of day at the beach and you are a competent windsurfer, you may decide to test your prowess, instead. Pick up a board, hoist the sail, wade into the water, start to catch the wind. Flow will come. Major flow.

The ramifications of flow wisdom are life changing. Follow the flow trail, and you will discover radiant new ways of being in the world.

If you wish to experience more calm and serenity, court stillness and the practice of letting go. If you wish to experience more flow, court autotelic action. Flow is not a lucky accident. Choose work that is autotelic for you. Choose hobbies that are autotelic. Flow comes as we dive into activity that facilitates full absorption.

Silence and flow. One path informs the other. Another paradox of life.

Travel both paths. Travel them with commitment and surrender. Moments will suddenly fly by, and they will last forever. You will know them with conscious appreciation. Your life will be less defined by your experience of time. You will more often, more fully be in the here and now. Glorious.

Explorations for Key #4: Make Time Stand Still

I don't know a single person who does not, at times, feel that life is moving too fast.

There are situations when the speed of life is beyond our control. The remainder of the time, it is about the choices we make. The benefits of slowing down are formidable. Slower time creates space. Space to think. Space to feel. Space to contemplate. And space to have a more conscious experience of how we actually spend our time. In slower time, we discover who we really are.

Slow-down by slow-down, we create a more sumptuously lived life. Here are three ways of reaping the benefits of slowing down, quiet time, and stillness.

Meditate

Find a practice that resonates with you. Practice is the routine that walks you into meditation. Meditation is the activity that calms your mind and opens the doors to a tangible experience of peace. A routine can be a set of specific breathing exercises, a guided meditation tape to which you listen, a mantra that you repeat, or gazing on an object such as a beautiful flower in your garden.

Considerations for a Beginner (inspired by a conversation with Frederick Tan)

Have no expectation of how meditation will benefit you. Allow the experience to be just as it is.

Try to meditate regularly in the same place, at the same time so meditation becomes a habit.

Get used to the ceremony of sitting down.

It can be helpful to meditate in a shared space or a class. You have a sense of not being alone. You have the comfort of a guide.

Comfort is paramount as you consider different seating options for meditation.

Make sure to hold your head and neck in alignment.

You will benefit from meditation at every stage of your practice, no matter how imperfect it may feel as you begin.

Considerations for a Seasoned Meditator

Contemplate the following questions as you meditate:

How may I further surrender myself as I sit still?

How may I continuously carry the spirit of meditation into every social encounter I have?

What are all the ways in which I know the divine as I sit still?

Experiment with Slow Activity

Most of us experience an abundance of speed, a scarcity of slowness. Our appreciation of life is enriched in immeasurable ways through the interplay of both states of being.

Create your slow experiments. Think of these experiments as playful adventures, not homework assignments. Approach them in a spirit of lighthearted fun.

Focus on one specific behavior, one aspect of your life, at a time. If you wish to take Will Self as a cue, start with your means of transportation. What would happen if you walk more frequently? Bicycle, perhaps? What would happen if you experiment with how you eat? Try slower meals, longer meals. What would happen if you perform daily tasks with a singular focus? Do single tasks instead of multitasking. What would happen if your lovemaking becomes a sweetly unhurried romp?

Pick your area of exploration. Pick an extended period of exploration, say a week or a month. This will allow you to settle into the experience of slowness. Do it once, and it is a diversion. Do it over a period of time, and your new behavior may evolve into a delicious new habit.

Unobligate Yourself

We have explored the personal benefits of unobligated time in this section. Now it's up to you. Just do it.

Pick a chunk of time in which you unobligate. An entire day is a great way to start. If that feels daunting, half a day will do. You decide.

Two considerations: Resist the temptation to justify or explain to dear ones why you are taking this time. If you do, you will be bombarded with their notions of what you should do with your time. And resist any temptation to plan in advance how you will spend this time. That is the radical part. You will be blessed with wonderful insights as you face your planning demons.

Give yourself completely to the moment-by-moment discovery of what shows up during unobligated time.

the

moment

continues

the moment continues

See if you can detect the bloom of the present moment in every moment, the ordinary ones, the "in-between" ones, even the hard ones.

—Jon Kabat-Zinn

Bloom.

The wisdom in Kabat-Zinn's tantalizing words tickles my fancy.[1] Yes, there is the possibility of bloom in every single moment, and it is up to you and me to detect it.

As you explore the tools and principles of this book, have a bit of fun experiencing the world around you with all of your senses. Tune into prajna wisdom as it reveals itself to you. Relish the energy within you and around you, and experience the joy of riding a wave or two. Bask in those days, hours, minutes when you allow time to stand still. Unobligate yourself a little. Settle into your moments of peace.

And along the way, beat by beat, detect the bloom.

I am quickly charmed by the easy bloom. The morning sun as it rises past the horizon line and sprinkles the ocean with light. The candlelit dinner with a person I love, when everything about the moment feels just right. The exhale when I complete a task on time, and the joy of my full creative absorption every step of the way.

The bloom that stirs me even more is the bloom of the unexpected place, the improbable moment. The gritty beauty of living in a rough-and-tumble Meatpacking District in Brooklyn, two blocks from the East River, before it was fashionable to do so.

The stillness as I stand bedside next to my dad, in his final days, while he breathes with a heaving heart, no longer able to communicate. The day you and I have the most piercing disagreement we have ever had, and then suddenly, out of nowhere, my love for you wells up inside.

Here is a bonus bloom detector for you.

Actors call it the "master gesture." It's the key to hidden treasures, to knowing another person beyond the limits of words.

Consider this possibility: Everyone we meet makes certain gestures that reveal to us the essence of who they are. The gesture we speak of is not deliberate. It is an unwitting quirk or an impulsive expression. When we catch the gesture, we catch a glimpse of the heart and soul of who that person truly is, behind the surface chatter and the social distractions.

The gesture is the bloom.

This is how some actors prepare for a role. They create a gesture, often a very small one, that reveals the essence of a character. The flick of a hand, a nervous stroke of the chin. They call it the "essential gesture," or the "master gesture," and they experiment with this gesture in rehearsal. Once the gesture "feels right" to the actor, it becomes integrated into the performance of the part.

Every time the actor uses this gesture, the deepest truth about that character gets divulged. We merely need to notice.

Real wisdom. Deep prajna. Revealed in a nanosecond.

Here's how this works in real life. Take my mom. I know my mother loves me a whole lot. This is her bloom. When I carry my suitcase toward the train on the crumbling old train platform in Bad Godesberg, the city where Mom lives, and I finally turn around, I see her standing on the other side of the platform looking toward me. I catch the wave of Mom's hand. It's quick. It's insistent. It's childlike. It looks like it doesn't ever wish to stop.

That wave, that hand. That is the depth of my mom's love for me.

My friend Jameson Maroncelli likes to dive into the pool at the Rainbow Bend Resort in Grassy Key. His diving technique is precise. But the second before Jameson dives he stops, steps up to his toes, holds the moment, focuses. Then he jumps. That pause, that moment of deliberate concentration, the sense of purpose in a simple dive. That is the essence of Jameson. His bloom.

Just as people have their bloom, places do as well—the spot, the view, the smell that captures the essence of an entire geography.

When I head from Miami to the beach, I make the crossing via the Julia Tuttle Causeway. "The beach" is Miami lingo for the City of Miami Beach. Seconds after the causeway lifts from the mainland it rises to an elevation above Biscayne Bay and then rapidly descends. As my car reaches this mini-peak, the view distends: Aventura and the Bay Harbor Islands and Surfside to the distant north, the entire glorious stretch of Miami Beach in front of me, the furtive Venetian islands in full view to the south, the mammoth skyline of downtown Miami and Brickell, the outline of the Rickenbacker Causeway that circles to a distant Key Biscayne.

The view disappears in seconds. It takes my breath away, every time.

This vista is the essence of my Miami. Sparkling sea. Lush little islands. A big sky. An unlimited universe. Bedazzling.

My heart jumps with joy. My Miami bloom.

The sudden view of a forgotten canal in Venice Beach. The skinny stray cat that dashes down the alley behind my house. The dolphin fin that arches out of the sea, dips away into the deep.

All bloom.

Moments are such a slippery and ephemeral thing. They come and go with the blink of an eye.

That is their beauty and their curse. Miss too many moments, and you miss your entire life.

Detect the bloom, and you catch the soul of a person, the spirit of a place.

What you really catch, of course, is your love of the world. The sordid and the sublime. The banal and the exceptional. The big transcendent love of it all.

That's a pretty nice catch, I say.

Keep catching.

notes

The Moment Begins

1. Jung, C. G. *Modern Man in Search of a Soul.* New York, NY: Harcourt, Brace & World, 1933.

2. Ouspensky, P. D. *In Search of the Miraculous.* San Diego, CA: Harcourt, 2001. P. D.

Ouspensky's best-selling book about the teachings of Gurdjieff.

3. Schiller, Marjorie, Bea Mah Holland, and Deanna Riley. *Appreciative Leaders: In the Eye of the Beholder.* Chagrin Falls, OH: Taos Institute, 2001.

4. Schacter, Daniel L. *Searching for Memory: The Brain, the Mind, and the Past.* New York, NY: Basic, 1996.

5. Heart Sutra. The earliest trace of the Heart Sutra was found at Horyuji Temple, Japan, dated 609 CE.

6. *The Garden of the Finzi-Continis.* Dir. Vittorio De Sica. Perf. Dominique Sanda, Helmut Berger, Fabio Testi, and Romolo Valli. Documento Film, 1970.

7. Brook, Peter. *The Empty Space: A Book About the Theatre: Deadly, Holy, Rough, Immediate.* New York, NY: Simon & Schuster, 1996.

8. Abramović, Marina. *Marina Abramović: The Artist Is Present.* 14 March–31 May 2010. Museum of Modern Art, New York, NY 10019.

9. Abramović, Marina. *Marina Abramović: 512 Hours.* 11 June–25 August 2014. Serpentine Galleries, Kensington Gardens, London W2 3XA.

10. Sulcas, Roslyn. "An Artist Fills Galleries with Emptiness: Marina Abramović Opens at Serpentine Gallery in London." *New York Times* online. 11 June 2014.

Key #1: Awaken the Senses

1. *True Lies.* Dir. James Cameron. Perf. Arnold Schwarzenegger and Jamie Lee Curtis. Twentieth Century Fox, 1994.

2. *Sunset Boulevard.* Dir. Billy Wilder. Perf. William Holden, Gloria Swanson, and Erich Von Stroheim. Paramount Pictures, 1950.

3. Brennan, Barbara Ann. *Hands of Light: A Guide to Healing Through the Human Energy Field.* Toronto, Canada: Bantam, 1988.

4. Huxley, Aldous. *The Doors of Perception.* New York, NY: Harper & Brothers, 1954.

Key #2: Crave Meaning

1. Spieth, Jordan. "Jordan Spieth: Sunday Interview 2015." Interview at Masters Press Conference. 12 April 2015.

2. Nin, Anaïs, and Gunther Stuhlmann. *The Diary of Anaïs Nin.* Vol. 1. San Diego, CA: Swallow/Harcourt Brace, 1966.

3. "Bruce Jenner—The Interview." Interview with Bruce Jenner by Diane Sawyer. *20/20*. ABC. 24 April 2015.

4. Frankl, Viktor E. *Man's Search for Meaning*. Boston, MA: Beacon, 2006.

5. Campbell, Joseph. *The Hero with a Thousand Faces*. Princeton, NJ: Princeton University Press, 1972.

6. Indian fable. Source unknown.

7. Fredrickson, Barbara. *Love 2.0: Creating Happiness and Health in Moments of Connection*. New York, NY: Plume, 2014. Print.

8. Stratton-Berkessel, Robyn. *Appreciative Inquiry for Collaborative Solutions: 21 Strength-Based Workshops*. San Francisco, CA: Jossey-Bass, 2010.

9. Fredrickson, *Love 2.0*.

Key #3: Wave-Ride Energy

1. Murray, W. H., and Robert Anderson. *The Scottish Himalayan Expedition*. London, UK: Dent, 1951. Murray credits Johann Wolfgang von Goethe as the inspiration for this quote.

2. Wolfe, Alexandra. "Scott Neeson: The Movie Executive Turned Philanthropist on Leaving

Hollywood for Cambodia." *Wall Street Journal.* 13 June 2015: C11.

3. Nowak, Achim. "What Survives." *Seneca Review: The Lyric Body.* Ed. David Weiss. Vol. 39/2–40/1. Geneva, Switzerland: Hobart and William Smith College, 2010. 85–99. Print. Some of this material was previously published in the *Seneca Review.*

4. Tuff, Antoinette. Interview with Anderson Cooper. CNN. Anderson Cooper 360, 22 August 2013.

Key #4: Make Time Stand Still

1. Simon, Paul. *The Sounds of Silence.* Simon & Garfunkel. Tom Wilson, 1964.

2. *Quiet Time.* Dir. Judy Greer. Perf. Judy Greer. *AOL.* 28 Apr. 2014.

3. Butterworth, Eric. *In the Flow of Life.* Unity Village, MO: Unity, 1994.

4. Durgananda, Swami. *The Heart of Meditation.* South Fallsburg, NY: SYDA Foundation, 2002.

5. Iyer, Pico. *The Art of Stillness: Adventures in Going Nowhere.* New York, NY: Simon & Schuster/TED, 2014.

6. Iyer, Pico. "The Art of Stillness." Interview by Krista Tippett. *On Being*. NPR. 4 June 2015.

7. McGrath, Charles. "A Literary Visitor Strolls in From the Airport." *New York Times*. 6 December 2006.

8. Honoré, Carl. *In Praise of Slowness: Challenging the Cult of Speed*. San Francisco, CA: Harper SanFrancisco, 2005.

9. Csikszentmihalyi, Mihaly. *Creativity: Flow and the Psychology of Discovery and Invention*. New York: HarperCollins, 1996.

The Moment Continues

1. Epigraph: Kabat-Zinn, Jon. *Wherever You Go, There You Are: Mindfulness Meditation in Everyday Life*. New York, NY: Hyperion, 1994.

index

about the author

Achim Nowak is an author, speaker, executive coach, and international authority on personal presence. His books Infectious: How to Connect Deeply and Unleash the Energetic Leader Within (Skyhorse Publishing/2013) and Power Speaking (Allworth Press/2004/also in German and Chinese) have become prized resources for entrepreneurs and Fortune 500 executives around the world. Influens, the international training and coaching firm Achim founded in 2004, helps leaders at every organizational level to show up more boldly and be more influential.

Achim has a checkered past. That is one of his finer assets.

It includes training performers at The Actors Institute in Manhattan, spending a decade on the faculty of New York University, leading transformational AIDS Mastery Week-ends in church basements and community centers through North America, and disappearing to the island of Tobago for a year. In Tobago Achim windsurfed, read every Graham Greene novel he could get his hands on, and mastered the art of doing nothing.

This book draws on all of these experiences, as well as a 20-year journey of exploring Hindu practices, Native American mythology, and the rewards of silence. Achim holds an M.A. in Organizational Psychology and International Relations from New York University. He and his work have been featured on 60 Minutes, Fox News, and NPR, in The New York Times and The Miami Herald. Achim's writing has been recognized with a PEN Syndicated Fiction Award, and his work for the Shimon Peres Centre for Peace, where he helmed a collaboration between Palestinian, Israeli and Jordanian theatre artists, was captured in the award-winning documentary "The Last Enemy."

Achim's popular weekly Energy Boost message is received by a wide circle of influencers around the globe.

Follow him @AchimNowak or visit themoment.expert.